# Teach Yourself
## VISUALLY™

# Golf

# Teach Yourself VISUALLY™

## Golf

Visual®

by Cheryl Anderson, Brian A. Crowell, and Tom Mackin

BICENTENNIAL
1807
WILEY
2007
BICENTENNIAL

Wiley Publishing, Inc.

For general information on our other products and services or to obtain technical support please contact our Customer Care Department within the U.S. at (800) 762-2974, outside the U.S. at (317) 572-3993 or fax (317) 572-4002.

Wiley also publishes its books in a variety of electronic formats. Some content that appears in print may not be available in electronic books. For more information about Wiley products, please visit our web site at www.wiley.com.

Library of Congress Control Number: 2007921819

ISBN: 978-0-470-09844-8

Printed in the United States of America

10   9   8   7   6   5   4   3   2   1

Book production by Wiley Publishing, Inc. Composition Services

Wiley Bicentennial Logo: Richard J. Pacifico

# Praise for the Teach Yourself VISUALLY Series

I just had to let you and your company know how great I think your books are. I just purchased my third Visual book (my first two are dog-eared now!) and, once again, your product has surpassed my expectations. The expertise, thought, and effort that go into each book are obvious, and I sincerely appreciate your efforts. Keep up the wonderful work!

*—Tracey Moore (Memphis, TN)*

I have several books from the Visual series and have always found them to be valuable resources.

*—Stephen P. Miller (Ballston Spa, NY)*

Thank you for the wonderful books you produce. It wasn't until I was an adult that I discovered how I learn—visually. Although a few publishers out there claim to present the material visually, nothing compares to Visual books. I love the simple layout. Everything is easy to follow. And I understand the material! You really know the way I think and learn. Thanks so much!

*—Stacey Han (Avondale, AZ)*

Like a lot of other people, I understand things best when I see them visually. Your books really make learning easy and life more fun.

*—John T. Frey (Cadillac, MI)*

I am an avid fan of your Visual books. If I need to learn anything, I just buy one of your books and learn the topic in no time. Wonders! I have even trained my friends to give me Visual books as gifts.

*—Illona Bergstrom (Aventura, FL)*

I write to extend my thanks and appreciation for your books. They are clear, easy to follow, and straight to the point. Keep up the good work! I bought several of your books and they are just right! No regrets! I will always buy your books because they are the best.

*—Seward Kollie (Dakar, Senegal)*

# Credits

**Acquisitions Editor**
Pam Mourouzis

**Copy Editor**
Mike Thomas

**Editorial Manager**
Christina Stambaugh

**Publisher**
Cindy Kitchel

**Vice President and Executive Publisher**
Kathy Nebenhaus

**Interior Design**
Kathie Rickard
Elizabeth Brooks

**Cover Design**
Jose Almaguer

**Photography**
Fred Vuich (unless otherwise noted)

**Photographic Assistant**
Michael Cohen

# About the Authors

**Cheryl Anderson** is the director of instruction at Wykagyl Country Club in New Rochelle, New York. She received the LPGA's 2006 National Teacher of the Year award and is one of *Golf for Women* magazine's 50 Top Women Teachers in America. Cheryl also is one of the best woman club pro competitors ever. In 2004 she earned the Metropolitan PGA Section Women's Player of the Year award for a record fifth consecutive season. She also was runner-up in the 2002 LPGA National Club Professional Championship and has competed in numerous LPGA Tour events over the past decade.

A graduate of Rutgers University, Cheryl is a Class A member of both the LPGA and the PGA of America. She has authored numerous instruction articles for *Golf for Women* magazine, *Met Golfer* magazine, and *Golf Digest Woman* magazine.

**Brian A. Crowell** has been helping students enjoy the game of golf since 1991. He has held the position of Head Golf Professional since 1997 and is currently employed at GlenArbor Golf Club in Bedford, New York.

In addition to his volunteer work for various charities and programs, Brian has served on the Education Committee of the Metropolitan PGA since 1996 and has been the Chairman since 2002, when he joined the section's Board of Directors. In 2003 he was awarded the prestigious Horton Smith Award for his outstanding contributions to golf education. In 2005 Brian was elected to the Executive Committee and currently serves as the 2nd Vice President of the Metropolitan Section.

Brian is a highly regarded instructor in the Metropolitan Section and beyond. He has given countless individual lessons and clinics and has authored numerous instructional articles. Brian's work has been featured in Donald Trump's book *The Best Golf Advice*

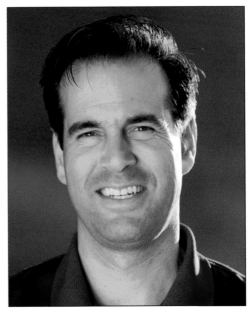

*I Ever Received* and in *The Secret of Golf* by George Peper. He has also contributed to many newspapers and magazines, including recent issues of *GOLF Magazine*. In 2003, National Consumers Research named Brian Crowell one of America's Best Instructors, and he is proud to have been selected as a Top 50 Kids Teacher for 2005 by *US Kids Golf*.

Brian has been seen in television commercials with Craig Stadler and can also be heard on the radio. He is the creator, host, and producer of "The Clubhouse," a golf radio show that can be heard Wednesdays from 6-7 pm on AM540 WLIE and AM1490 WGCH. The show can also be accessed online at www.wgch.com, and at www.met.pga.com.

A proud father and husband, Brian loves to spend time with his wife, Wendy, and their three children, Kevin, Casey, and Christina. The Crowell family lives in Bedford Hills, New York.

**Tom Mackin** has worked as an associate editor at *GOLF Magazine* and as a contributing editor for *The World of Hibernia, Hudson County Magazine,* and Zagat's *America's Top Golf Courses.* A frequent contributor on golf and travel to many national and international publications, he has written for *Travel and Leisure GOLF, LINKS* Magazine, *NICKLAUS* Magazine, *Golf World, The Met Golfer, Pebble Beach Magazine, Town & Country,* the *New York Times,* and *New Jersey Monthly.* He is a native of Bayonne, New Jersey, and a graduate of Rutgers University.

# Acknowledgments

**Brian Crowell:**
I would like to thank my family for their patience and support, GlenArbor Golf Club both for their encouragement and for the use of their beautiful facility for photography, Nike and Titleist for product support, and my co-authors.

**Cheryl Anderson:**
Special thanks to...
My parents, Henry and Geraldine, for their unconditional support of my career in golf, my brother Kurt for his sense of humor on the course, and my grandparents for introducing me to the game during our summers in Lake Placid, New York.
My coaches: Mike Bender for sharing his extraordinary knowledge of the golf swing with me, and John Elliott for infecting me with his enthusiasm for teaching.

Fred Griffin at the Grand Cypress Academy of Golf for allowing me to work on my game at what I believe is the finest practice facility in the country. It also has allowed me to watch the best players in the world work on their game and to understand the patience and perseverance that it takes to play at the highest level.

Pia Nilsson and Lynn Marriott for encouraging me to teach each person as an individual, and Dr. Rick Jensen for sharing his vast knowledge of athletic training methods.

Gene Borek for giving me advice on how to prepare to play my best and for sharing his short game secrets.

Skip Latella and Jeff Kaminski, who have helped me get my body in shape to make the golf swing that I wanted while also helping many of my students be able to play better by improving their strength and flexibility.

The wonderful members at Wykagyl Country Club, Metropolis Country Club, and Rolling Hills Country Club who have supported me for the past 15 years.

My husband, Lorin, for being the best caddie both on and off the golf course. You have done everything you could to help me succeed. You have shagged tens of thousands of practice balls for me at the end of many long days, and you have patiently sat through hundreds of videos of my students' swings when I was learning to teach to help me see things clearly.

Finally, to my beautiful new daughter, Callie Margaret Anderson, for helping me smile and laugh more than I ever have before.

Cheryl's clothing was provided by Fairway & Greene, her clubs and balls were provided by Callaway Golf, and her shoes are from Etonic.

**Tom Mackin:**
I'd like to thank Lorin Anderson and Marilyn Allen for bringing me to this project, Cheryl Anderson and Brian Crowell for sharing their knowledge and patiently answering endless questions, Fred Vuich and Michael Cohen for getting the pictures, and Pam Mourouzis and the Wiley staff for making it all happen. I'd also like to dedicate my effort with love and thanks to my parents, Tom Mackin, Sr., and Mary Mackin, for introducing me to golf and encouraging me to follow my dreams, and to my uncle Peter McVeigh for taking me out on my first 18-hole course and showing me the way to play.

Thanks also go to Janeen Driscoll at Pinehurst, Jane Fader at the World Golf Hall of Fame, Tiffany Nelson at TPC Scottsdale, Beth O'Reilly at Whistling Straits, Valerie Ramsey at Pebble Beach, Kristin Schaner at Bandon Dunes, Richard Snowten at the Orlando/Orange County Convention & Visitors Bureau, and the South Carolina Department of Parks, Recreation and Tourism for sharing photos of their respective destinations. Finally, thanks to Marcella Durand for photo research.

# Table of Contents

 **chapter 1** An Introduction to Golf

 **chapter 2** Equipment

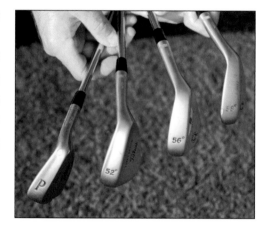

# chapter 3   Getting Set: Your Grip and Stance

# chapter 4   The Iron Swing

## chapter 5  Driving

## chapter 6  Chipping and Pitching

## chapter 7   **Bunker Shots**

## chapter 8   **Putting**

# chapter 9 At the Course

# chapter 10 Troubleshooting and Tricky Shots

 **chapter 11** **Improving Your Game**

# chapter 1

# An Introduction to Golf

Welcome to the often fascinating, sometimes frustrating, and almost always fun game of golf. It is a sport that can be played for a lifetime, yet can never be mastered completely. Some call it a good walk spoiled, but they probably have never experienced the thrill of hitting a ball high into the air in exactly the right direction, or the pleasure of making a long putt for a birdie. Doing either of those things takes a fair bit of learning, since golf is a complicated game. But put forth a patient effort, and positive results will eventually follow. This book gives you the basics needed to learn not only how to play the game, but also how to enjoy it.

# The History of the Game

Like almost every other sport, golf has a long and storied history. Here is a quick overview of the game's development.

## THE GAME OF GOLF IS BORN

No single person is credited with developing the game of golf. For a game strictly defined by rules, even the exact location of its beginnings is somewhat murky. Countries such as France, China, and Holland have all laid claim to inventing the sport, but it is Scotland, a country of some 5 million people, that is universally looked upon as the birthplace of golf. According to the United States Golf Association, "Some scholars suggest that the Dutch game of *kolf*, played with a stick and ball on frozen canals in the wintertime, was brought by Dutch sailors to the east coast of Scotland (in the 14th or 15th century), where it was transferred to the public linkslands and eventually became the game known today."

Indeed, no country is more proudly associated with the sport than Scotland, where you will find some of the finest courses in the world, including the famed Old Course in the town of St. Andrews, where golf has been played since at least the 16th century. The first

*The St. Andrews clubhouse and Swilcan Bridge.*
*Photo credit: John R. Johnson/golfphotos.com.*

official rules of golf were formed in 1744 an hour south in Edinburgh, and the St. Andrews Society of Golfers (now known as the Royal & Ancient Golf Club, whose imposing clubhouse overlooks the Old Course) was founded a decade later.

## GOLF REACHES THE UNITED STATES

Scottish and British golf professionals traveled to the United States in the late 1800s, bringing with them an intimate knowledge of the game along with course-building skills. The first official club—named St. Andrew's Golf Club, naturally—was formed in Yonkers, New York, in 1888. The United States Golf Association, founded in 1894, is based in Far Hills, New Jersey, and runs numerous national championships for amateur and professional golfers of all ages, oversees the game's rules (in conjunction with the Royal & Ancient Golf Club), and coordinates the handicap system (see page 159). One year after its formation, the first 18-hole course in the United States, called the Chicago Golf Club, opened.

As the game's popularity began to grow, the Professional Golfers Association of America was formed in 1916, while the Ladies Professional Golf Association was formed in 1950. As cities and towns sprouted in the west and suburban sprawl started to occur around major metropolitan areas, golf course construction increased as well. Private country clubs were built for the rich and famous, while affordably priced municipal courses provided outlets for less affluent golfers.

## INDIVIDUAL PLAYERS GRAB HEADLINES AND DOMINATE BROADCASTS

Legendary players contributed to the growth of the game in America during the 20th century, drawing a share of the public's attention from more established sports such as baseball, basketball, and football. When 20-year-old amateur Francis Ouimet won the 1913 U.S. Open at the Country Club in Brookline, Massachusetts, he became the first star in American golf circles. The many wins of Bobby Jones dominated the sports headlines in the 1920s and 1930s, followed by Byron Nelson, Sam Snead, and Ben Hogan in the 1940s and 1950s. The introduction of the highly personable Arnold Palmer took the game to a whole new level of popularity in the 1960s, with his devoted fans forming "Arnie's Army." He soon found competition from an Ohio youngster named Jack Nicklaus (and nicknamed the "Golden Bear"), who would go on to compile the greatest winning record in the history of the game. Those records are now firmly in the sights of Tiger Woods, who started playing golf at the age of three and won his first major professional tournament—the Masters—in 1997 at the mere age of 21.

*Bobby Jones. Photo credit: Hulton Archive/Getty Images.*

On the women's side, the cast of stars is no less grand. The all-around athlete Babe Didrikson Zaharias drew plenty of attention with her tournament wins in the late 1940s and into the 1950s, followed by superb players like Patty Berg, Louise Suggs, Mickey Wright, and Kathy Whitworth. The success of Nancy Lopez in the late 1970s reignited interest in the women's game, while Annika Sorenstam from Sweden is universally acclaimed as the world's best female golfer from the 1990s and into the 21st century.

The course design business has featured increasingly well-known professionals as well, with architects like Robert Trent Jones, Sr. (whose sons Rees and Robert, Jr., are highly regarded today), a dominant figure for almost five decades. The 1980s and 1990s marked a golf construction boom, with modern course designers like Pete Dye, Tom Fazio, Jack Nicklaus, and Tom Doak all leaving their mark with layouts in every corner of the United States, just like their Scottish and British counterparts did nearly a century before.

Television helped introduce the game to a national audience. In 1953, television helped introduce the game to a national audience when the first broadcast of a tournament to the entire country. Today, a whole cable television channel (appropriately named the Golf Channel) is devoted to the sport.

## GOLF EQUIPMENT EVOLVES

Equipment used to play the game has evolved over time into a huge business. In 2002, golfers spent $4.7 billion on equipment (clubs, balls, bags, gloves, shoes, etc.), according to the National Golf Foundation. The biggest change that came about during the 1980s was the introduction of metal woods. Technological advances continue today, resulting in lighter and more forgiving clubs along with balls that travel farther than ever before—all designed to help people enjoy a game that started on frozen ponds in one small country and is now played in every part of the world.

# Important Tournaments

The four best-known events on the professional golf calendar are collectively referred to as the majors.

## The Majors

### THE MASTERS

Played at Augusta National Golf Club in Augusta, Georgia, the Masters started in 1934. The tournament is played every April on a private course built by legendary golfer Bobby Jones (see page 7) and prolific course designer Alister MacKenzie. The winner earns a coveted green jacket.

### THE U.S. OPEN

The national championship run by the United States Golf Association (USGA) has been played at a different site in the U.S. each summer since 1895. Look for this tournament, which attracts top players from all over the world, in June.

### THE BRITISH OPEN

First played in 1860, this event is held at one of a rotation of courses in Scotland and England each July. It, too, is open to players from around the globe.

### THE PGA CHAMPIONSHIP

Run by the Professional Golfers Association of America since 1916, this event is held annually in late summer at different courses around the United States.

Over the years, numerous events have been considered "majors" in women's professional golf, but since 2001 the following tournaments have fallen into that category:

- The Kraft Nabisco Championship
- The McDonald's LPGA Championship
- The U.S. Open
- The British Open

Jack Nicklaus makes his final putt on the 18th green at the British Open Championship, July 15, 1978. Photo credit: PGA Tour Images.

## Team Tournaments

The highest level of competition for non-professionals is the men's and women's U.S. Amateur (also run by the USGA), which uses both a stroke play and match play format (see the Glossary) to determine a champion.

There are also professional team events that are played on a biannual basis at different courses in the U.S. and abroad, such as:

- The Ryder Cup (the United States versus Europe)
- The Presidents Cup (the United States versus the rest of the world)
- The Solheim Cup (United States women versus European women)
- The Curtis Cup (United States amateur women versus amateurs from Ireland and Great Britain)

# Legendary Players

There have been a number of male and female players on the PGA and LPGA Tours whose skills and records transcend the eras in which they played. Their achievements continue to form the standard for modern-day golfers.

## Men

### BOBBY JONES (1902–1971)

This Georgia native founded the Augusta National Golf Club and the Masters tournament in his home state. He won the U.S. Open four times and the British Open three times, and is the only golfer to have won the four events that at the time formed the Grand Slam (in 1930, when he won the U.S. Amateur, British Amateur, British Open, and U.S. Open). After that triumph, he retired and worked as a lawyer, wrote books, and made golf instruction films, leaving a mark on the game matched by few.

### BYRON NELSON (1912–2006)

The highlight of this golfer's 11-year career came in 1945, when he won 18 tournaments, including 11 in a row. He also won five majors, including two Masters titles and two PGA Championships. The Fort Worth, Texas native—who retired at age 34—was revered both during his playing days and afterward as a true gentleman.

### BEN HOGAN (1912–1997)

This Texas native won two Masters, four U.S. Opens, one British Open, and two PGA Championships. Known as one of the best ball strikers ever, Hogan's legendary work ethic earned him tremendous respect, as did his comeback from a car accident in 1949, after which he won six majors.

### ARNOLD PALMER (1929–)

Palmer, a Pennsylvania native, won four Masters, two British Opens, and one U.S. Open. He is known for his swashbuckling style and his connection with his fans, who came to be known as "Arnie's Army." He was the first golfer to maximize commercial product endorsements, increasing his public recognition. He also built a thriving golf course design business.

### JACK NICKLAUS (1940–)

This Ohio native, nicknamed the Golden Bear, is the most successful golfer of all time. He won six Masters, four U.S. Opens, three British Opens, five PGA Championships, and two U.S. Amateurs. Nicklaus took the golf spotlight from Palmer in the 1960s via countless wins thanks to superior distance and clutch putting. In 1986, at age 46, he won his final Masters and perhaps his most memorable victory.

### TIGER WOODS (1975–)

A California native, Woods has won four Masters, two U.S. Opens, three British Opens, three PGA Championships, and three consecutive U.S. Amateurs. Groomed for a golf career by his father, Woods has exceeded all expectations to become a dominant figure in the game today, combining playing ability, physical fitness, and mental toughness that will likely lead him to break most, if not all, of the game's most important records.

*Tiger Woods wins the 2000 U.S. Open.*
*Photo credit: PGA Tour Images.*

***CONTINUED ON NEXT PAGE***

## Women

### BABE DIDRIKSON ZAHARIAS (1911–1956)

This pioneering female athlete competed in the 1932 Olympics and won two gold medals in track and field before taking up golf at age 35, going on to win the U.S. and British Amateurs. She was a founding member of the LPGA and won three U.S. Women's Opens.

### MICKEY WRIGHT (1935–)

This California native won four U.S. Women's Opens and three LPGA Championships among her 82 wins on the Tour. Owner of one of the most beautiful swings the game has ever seen, Wright is the only LPGA player to have held all four major titles simultaneously and won 13 events in 1963.

### KATHY WHITWORTH (1939–)

This Texas native won 88 times on the LPGA Tour and was the first woman to compile $1 million in career earnings. She captured six major titles, was a seven-time LPGA Player of the Year, and was the LPGA's leading money winner eight times.

### NANCY LOPEZ (1957–)

A New Mexico native, Lopez won nine tournaments, including five in a row, during a memorable rookie season on the LPGA Tour in 1978. She went on to win 48 times, including three majors, and captained the victorious U.S. team in the 2005 Solheim Cup.

### ANNIKA SORENSTAM (1970–)

This native of Sweden has won three U.S. Women's Open titles, won more LPGA Tournaments (18) than any other player in the 1990s, and has won 69 times on LPGA Tour overall through the 2006 season. Recognized as the most dominant player in the game, in 2003 Sorenstam played in a PGA Tour event in Texas, the first woman to do so since Didrikson Zaharias in 1945.

*Annika Sorenstam hits from the 13th tee during the final round of the 2005 Merrill Lynch Skins Game at Trilogy Golf Club in La Quinta. Photo credit: PGA Tour Images.*

Golf is a simple game in theory. Hit a small, round ball with a club. Go find it. Then hit it again (and again and again) until it goes into a hole in the ground. Complete that process for 18 holes. Except it wasn't always that way.

Until the late 19th century, the number of holes on golf courses varied from fewer than ten to more than 20. The Old Course at St. Andrews consisted of 11 holes that went from the clubhouse to the end of a piece of land. Golfers would turn around and play the holes again, coming back to where they started, meaning that a round of golf consisted of 22 holes. In the late 18th century, several of those holes were combined to form nine holes, resulting in the now standard total of 18 holes being played to complete a round.

## Quick Playing Tips for Beginners

- Play from the proper set of tees. Each hole has multiple sets of tees that shorten or lengthen the hole—play the ones most appropriate for your skill level. If you aren't sure, play a more forward set of tees. You'll enjoy the course more.

- Always maintain your pace of play; do not unnecessarily delay the golfers in your own group or the group behind you. For example, if your strokes are double the par for a hole, pick up your ball and move on to the next hole.

- Be quiet. Making excess noise on a golf course is in poor taste, especially while another player is making a swing.

- Play safe. Never swing a club when someone is standing near you, and always make sure that no one is in the intended path of your shot.

- Take lessons. Rare is the player who can build a solid, repeatable swing without taking lessons. While it involves both a financial investment and a time commitment, learning the basics correctly will save you a priceless amount of frustration.

- Have fun. Yes, the object of the game is to get the ball into the hole in as few as strokes as possible, but if doing that is boring and overly serious, why bother? Respect the game, but enjoy it as well.

***CONTINUED ON NEXT PAGE***

## Quick Rules Tips for Beginners

Being true to the spirit of the game—playing by the rules—is required of all golfers no matter what their skill level. And there are rules to follow, of course. The latest edition of *The Rules of Golf,* published by the United States Golf Association and the Royal & Ancient Golf Society, is a whopping 268 pages long. Although as a beginner your main goals are to learn the game and have fun, it's also important to understand the rules.

Just as with any new activity, many people are intimidated by not knowing what to do when they play golf for the first time. While different courses have their own specific rules and regulations, some basic guidelines are common to all golf courses. Knowing these guidelines should put you at ease for your first visit. Chapter 9 outlines specific rules situations, but here are five quick tips:

- Many beginners often miss the ball entirely. Taking a swing with the intent to make contact with the ball does count as a stroke, and you must mark your score-card accordingly.

- You may tee the ball up only within the designated area of the tee box for each hole.

- When you lose a ball, you must take a penalty stroke as part of your score for that hole.

- You may touch your ball only when you are teeing it up and on the putting surface when you are either cleaning it (after having marked its location) or picking it after it has entered the hole.

- You must remove the flagstick from the hole prior to attempting putts on the green. If the ball hits the flagstick while it's still in the hole, you incur a two-stroke penalty.

## FACT

If any of your fellow players quote a movie while playing, it's likely to be *Caddyshack.* The 1980 comedy starring Bill Murray, Rodney Dangerfield, Chevy Chase, and Ted Knight was an instant classic among golfers for its lowbrow but undeniably funny look behind the scenes at the fictional Bushwood Country Club. At some point during some round on some course, you will hear a fellow golfer utter a line or two from the movie. Watch this flick and you can respond accordingly!

You will come across several different types of golf courses, which vary both in the types of holes they feature and in their policies regarding whom can play there.

- **Regulation:** A regulation course is considered a full-sized course. It can consist of nine or 18 holes with full-length par-threes, par-fours, and par-fives (see page 13).
- **Executive:** An executive course can be made up of nine or 18 holes, but the holes are shorter than on a regulation course.
- **Private:** A private course is open only to members.
- **Semi-private:** A semi-private course offers both memberships and tee times for non-members.
- **Public:** A public course, also called a daily-fee course or a municipal course if owned and/or managed by local officials, is open to anyone.
- **Pitch and putt:** A pitch-and-putt course is a nine- or 18-hole course with very short holes, most under 100 yards. These courses are generally open to the public.
- **Miniature:** You use only your putter on a miniature golf course, which usually has at least nine holes and numerous fun obstacles (windmills, clown's mouths, and so on) blocking your path to the hole.

There are also two main styles of courses:

- **Links:** A course usually built on treeless, sandy soil alongside (or "linked" to) the sea. Some courses use this description if the land is wide open and devoid of trees, but authenticity is lacking if the course is not near the sea. The Old Course at St. Andrews, shown here, is a good example of a traditional links course.
- **Parkland:** A course in which golf holes are defined by trees on both sides.

*The Old Course at St. Andrews. Photo credit: John R. Johnson/golfphotos.com.*

**FACT**

According to the National Golf Foundation, at the end of 2005, there were 16,052 facilities containing at least one golf course in the United States, and 11,680 of those were open to the public. The states with the most golf facilities included:

- Florida (1,075)
- California (928)
- Texas (848)
- Michigan (843)
- New York (824)

# The Parts of a Golf Course

Although courses do vary in type, the vast majority feature common elements.

## Course Elements

- **Tee box:** The area from which you hit your first shot on each hole. Most courses feature multiple sets of tees to accommodate golfers of different skill levels. The back tee boxes are used by only the best golfers; these tees extend the course to its longest possible yardage. The middle tee boxes are used by most average golfers. The forward tee boxes are used by most female and senior golfers. (All golfers play to the same green no matter which tee box they have used.)

- **Fairway:** The closely mown stretch of turf between the tee and the green.

- **Cart path:** The formal path throughout the course for golf carts to drive on. Keep your cart on this path unless otherwise instructed by course officials.

- **Rough:** High, often thick grass that borders the fairway and surrounds the green.

- **Bunker:** A hazard usually filled with sand (but sometimes grass) found mostly around greens but also on fairways.

- **Water hazard:** A pond, lake, river, or stream found in the middle or to the side of a hole.

- **Fringe:** The closely mown turf that encircles the putting surface; fringe grass is slightly higher than the grass of the green itself.

- **Green:** The designated putting surface for each hole, where the flagstick and cup are located.

- **Out-of-bounds area:** An area indicated by white stakes that is considered out of play. If a ball is hit into an out-of-bounds area, a one-stroke penalty is incurred, and your next swing must be taken from where your last shot was played.

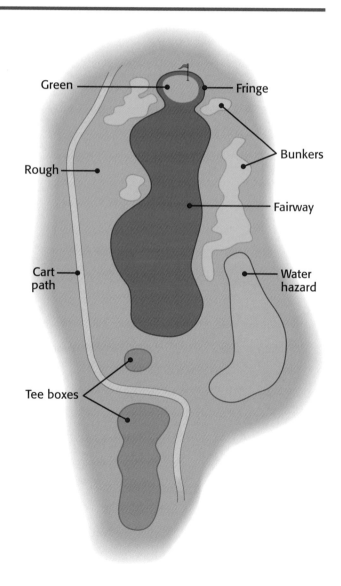

## Types of Holes

The main factor that defines a type of hole is its par. That number reflects the number of strokes it should take an experienced golfer to complete the hole. There are three types of holes: par-threes, par-fours, and par-fives. The yardage of each hole determines the par.

The following distances are general guidelines for the lengths of each type of hole. (The lengths of holes played by professionals vary from these guidelines.)

- **Par-three:** Up to 210 yards for women and up to 250 yards for men
- **Par-four:** 211–400 yards for women and 251–470 yards for men
- **Par-five:** 401–575 yards for women and 471–690 yards for men

You may also hear the term *dogleg* used to describe a par-four or par-five. That term refers to the shape of the hole, which usually bends fairly dramatically to either the right (as shown here) or the left.

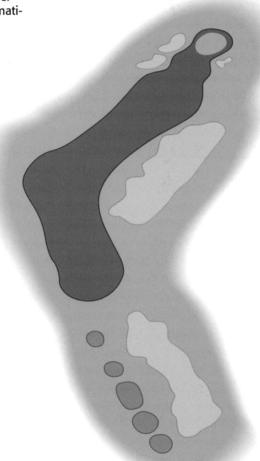

## FACT

The longest course in the United States is found in Bolton, Massachusetts. The private Pines Course at The International is 8,325 yards long. The fifth hole is a 715-yard par-five; there is also a 277-yard par-three. The 18th hole is a mere 656 yards.

# Keeping Score

While there is often great pleasure, and much less pressure, in playing a relaxed round of golf without keeping score, compiling the numbers is what enables you to measure your improvement. It's quite simple: Each attempt to hit the ball counts as one stroke, whether it's a 250-yard drive or a 6-inch putt. Add up the number of strokes you take from your first tee shot to your last putt, and that's your score.

Beyond simple numbers, golf scores have names that you should know.

## Scoring Terminology

- **Ace:** The ultimate shot—a hole-in-one.
- **Double eagle:** Three strokes below par for the hole (for example, a 2 on a par-five).
- **Eagle:** Two strokes below par (for example, a 3 on par-five).
- **Birdie:** One stroke below par (for example, a 3 on a par-four).
- **Par:** The number of strokes an experienced player should require to finish a hole (for example, a 4 on a par-four).
- **Bogey:** One stroke above par (for example, a 5 on a par-four).
- **Double bogey:** Two strokes above par (for example, a 6 on a par-four).
- **Snowman:** A score of eight. Look at the number and you'll figure out why this term is used.

Every course provides a scorecard free of charge so that you can keep track of the strokes you take. Chapter 9 explains how to use the scorecard and what it can help you with in addition to tallying your score.

## FACT

According to the National Golf Foundation, the average score on an 18-hole regulation golf course was 97 (95 for men and 106 for women) in 2004. The average handicap among the 21 percent of golfers who maintain one was 15 for men and 23 for women. See Chapter 9 for more on handicaps.

Go to any driving range and you will quickly learn why golf is such a humbling game. You will see all sorts of people using all types of swings with a wide variety of results.

As a beginner, your immediate goals should be to learn as much as you can about setting up to the ball and developing a good grip. After that, you will begin to understand how the club should move during the swing and the differences between the clubs you will be using. All that will help you get comfortable with the golf swing.

Try to be a sponge and soak up as much of this information as possible. Being realistic is important—it takes time before you are ready to go out and play on a course. The amount of time will be different for everyone. Going out unprepared or without more-experienced companions will not help you enjoy the game.

Take the example of one woman who received a lesson from the professional at the club her husband joined. The lesson marked the very first time she had ever touched a golf club. A few hours after the brief lesson, the professional who gave her that lesson was amazed to see her out on the course trying to play golf with her husband. The woman was completely frustrated, as was her husband, who was desperately trying to explain everything she was doing wrong. The woman never played golf again. Unrealistic expectations ruined the game for her.

So while that one perfect shot that sends your ball flying through the air on the driving range may have you hooked, remember that learning to play golf takes time. You can always get better. The best players in the world all have coaches who continually work with them on their swings. And they play every day. If you play only a few times a year, don't expect to shoot in the 70s—expect to have fun, continue learning, and try to improve each time you play.

# Why You Should Play

Why play golf? For one thing, you won't be alone on the course. According to the National Golf Foundation, in 2005 an estimated 12.5 million adult golfers in the United States played at least eight times a year, with the average being 37 times. Of that 12.5 million, 10.2 million were male and 2.3 million were female. But then there are as many reasons to play golf as there are types of swings.

## Reasons to Love Golf

- You're outdoors enjoying the fresh air, probably in a scenic location.
- Golf can be a part-time or full-time hobby, or even an entire lifestyle for those who move into homes that are part of golf course communities.
- You can play on the same courses as the game's greatest players. You'll pay a lot to do so, but you can, unlike other sports where the fields of play are off-limits.
- Plenty of business is conducted on golf courses, whether it's a one-on-one client meeting or a corporate outing.
- Golf can be a learning experience that you can share with friends or family.
- Golf is a competitive outlet for athletes whose bodies may be worn down from playing other sports like basketball or tennis. Golf is essentially a non-impact sport, where the post-round discussion usually focuses on the shots you made (and missed) rather than the aches and pains you got from playing.
- If you walk while playing, you'll be taking a 4- to 6-mile stroll over 18 holes, even if you keep all your shots in the fairway. It's not running a marathon, but it sure is better for you than sitting in a recliner for four and a half hours.

Because golf is played around the globe, learning how to play, and then traveling to do so, can open up entirely new worlds. Being randomly paired up with strangers on the first tee often leads to vacation-long, if not lifelong, friendships, thanks to golf being the common link that overcomes language and cultural barriers. Golf trips are usually tremendous bonding experiences and can provide great memories, not to mention plenty of laughs.

Here are a few points to consider when planning a golf trip.

## Take Your Game on the Road

### YEARLY MAINTENANCE

To maintain vibrant green fairways and smooth putting greens, many courses undergo processes called *overseeding* and *aeration*. The former can close a course for up two weeks (especially in desert climates like Arizona, where overseeding usually takes place in late September or early October), while the latter leaves greens rough and bumpy for five to seven days. Call the courses at your destination to find out when they schedule these procedures.

### SEASONS

The month of July might mean great weather for New England, but it can be unbearably hot in Arizona. Research the weather patterns of your destination before picking a time to visit.

### TOUR OPERATORS

Traveling with a foursome is one thing, but larger groups require much more coordination that an experienced golf tour operator can handle smoothly, especially if your group is traveling overseas to play the historic and legendary courses of Scotland and Ireland.

### LOCAL CUSTOMS

Every course has its own set of rules, regulations, and traditions. Read up on your destination and the courses you plan to play to find out how they do things there. Doing so is even more important overseas, where cultural differences can be particularly striking.

## FACT

According to the National Golf Foundation, golfers spend about $26.1 billion a year on golf travel, 75 percent of which goes to the hotel, transportation, and food and beverage industries.

*CONTINUED ON NEXT PAGE*

## Favorite U.S. Destinations

### SCOTTSDALE, ARIZONA

Enjoy desert golf at its finest here in the Valley of the Sun. Fairways roll out on the desert floor like bright green carpets, while cacti stand guard along the fairways. Courses like We-Ko-Pa, Troon North, Grayhawk, and the TPC of Scottsdale can keep you busy for weeks at a time. Find more information at www.scottsdalecvb.com.

*TPC Scottsdale Stadium Course, hole #16.*

## PEBBLE BEACH, CALIFORNIA

This world-famous resort, two hours south of San Francisco on the Pacific coast, always lives up to its dramatic setting. It's worth the splurge for a once in-a-lifetime round on these famous links (although you do have to stay at one of the resort's hotels to get a tee time). Also worth playing are Spanish Bay, Spyglass, and Poppy Hills, all located within the secluded Del Monte Forest, whose natural beauty never fails to awe visitors. Find travel information at www.pebblebeach.com.

*Pebble Beach Golf Links, hole #7. Photo credit: Joann Dost. Reproduced by Permission of Pebble Beach Company.*

**CONTINUED ON NEXT PAGE**

## ORLANDO, FLORIDA

There are more than just Disney characters here in this Sunshine State city. Bring your clubs to play courses like Arnold Palmer's Bay Hill, ChampionsGate, Orange County National, and Grand Cypress. There are even four courses at Walt Disney World, where Mickey Mouse hats serve as tee markers. Find travel information at www.orlandoinfo.com.

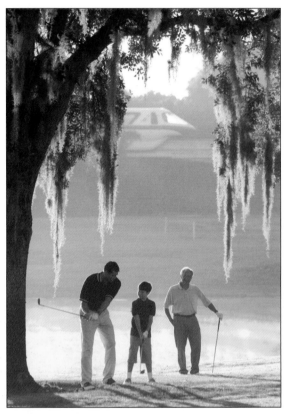

*Walt Disney World Resort Golf. Photo credit: Orlando/Orange County Convention & Visitors Bureau, Inc.*

## WORLD GOLF VILLAGE, FLORIDA

The World Golf Hall of Fame is located in historic St. Augustine, just south of Jacksonville. You can find memorabilia and artifacts from the game's history as well as learn about golf's greatest players. There's also an IMAX theater, shops, restaurants, accommodations, and two golf courses: King & Bear (designed by Arnold Palmer and Jack Nicklaus) and Slammer & Squire (designed by Sam Snead and Gene Sarazen). For more information, go to www.wghof.com.

*The World Golf Hall of Fame.*

## HAWAII

The views from the fairways in the Hawaiian islands are distracting, but then you're not visiting the Aloha State to worry about your scores. From Kapalua on Maui to Mauna Kea on the Big Island and Poipu Bay on Kauai, the choices for golfers are endless. Find travel information at www.gohawaii.com.

*Kapalua's Plantation Course, hole #8. Photo credit: John R. Johnson/golfphotos.com.*

**CONTINUED ON NEXT PAGE**

## PINEHURST, NORTH CAROLINA

The famous No. 2 Course at the Pinehurst Resort gets all the attention both for its designer, Donald Ross, and its devilish, hard-to-putt greens, but numerous other courses (including eight others at this resort alone) are worth playing here, including Pine Needles (the site of multiple U.S. Women's Opens), Mid-Pines, and Tobacco Road. Find travel information at www.homeofgolf.com.

*Pinehurst No. 2 Course, hole #5. Photo credit: ®Pinehurst, Inc. All rights reserved.*

## BANDON DUNES, OREGON

Three magnificent courses on the remote southern Oregon Coast have drawn rave reviews since the moment they opened: the original Bandon Dunes course, followed by Pacific Dunes and then Bandon Trails. Find travel information at www. bandondunesgolf.com.

*Pacific Dunes, hole #11. Photo credit: Wood Sabold.*

***CONTINUED ON NEXT PAGE***

## HILTON HEAD/MYRTLE BEACH/KIAWAH ISLAND, SOUTH CAROLINA

These three coastal locations are mini-Meccas for traveling golfers. You can play a PGA Tour course in Hilton Head (Harbour Town), a world-famous venue on Kiawah Island (the Ocean Course), or a classic Robert Trent Jones, Sr. design in Myrtle Beach (the Dunes Golf and Beach Club). All three locations have many other quality courses to choose from. Find travel information at golf.discoversouthcarolina.com.

*Kiawah Island Ocean Course. Photo credit: South Carolina Department of Parks, Recreation & Tourism, DiscoverSouthCarolina.com.*

## WHISTLING STRAITS, WISCONSIN

An hour north of Milwaukee, Kohler Resort boasts four distinct courses highlighted by the namesake layout that hosted the 2004 PGA Championship. Whistling Straits and the Irish Course are adjacent to Lake Michigan, while Blackwolf Run and the Meadows are inland but no less fun. Find travel information at www.destinationkohler.com.

# 2

# Equipment

No piece of golf equipment is more important than the clubs you use to hit the ball. There are comfortable shoes, appropriate clothing, and all sorts of cool gadgets to consider, but you can't do anything on the course without your clubs. This chapter discusses all the types of golf clubs you will need and their purposes, plus clothing, shoes, bags and carts to carry your clubs, and other essential and not-so-essential gadgets.

# Clubs

Today's technology enables people to hit a golf ball farther than ever before. It means that golf clubs are more expensive (and cooler-looking) as well. Clubs differ in size, shape, length, and purpose. Each club is designed to hit the ball a certain yardage, a distance that is affected by many factors. This section discusses each part of a golf club and the types of clubs you should consider including in your bag.

## THE DRIVER AND WOODS

The driver and the woods are the longest clubs and usually have the largest clubheads. They also hit the ball the farthest when swung properly.

Drivers, which are almost always used to hit the ball off the tee, vary in length, clubhead size, and loft. While many professionals use drivers with lofts of less than 10 degrees, beginners should consider a greater loft, which helps get the ball into the air more easily. In general, men should look for a loft of 9.5 to 12.0 degrees, and women 12.0 to 15.5 degrees. As for the driver's clubhead size, the bigger, the better. Having a large clubface increases your margin for less-than-perfect hits, where even shots struck off-center tend to go farther and somewhat straighter than in the past, when clubheads were smaller.

Fairway woods look similar to drivers—the main difference is the size of the clubhead (fairway woods are smaller) and the loft of the clubface (fairway woods have a higher degree of loft). Although they're called *woods* because the clubhead used to be made of wood, most woods today have clubheads made of metal; they are sometimes referred to as *metal woods*. Woods come in numbers that ascend with the amount of loft the clubface has: 2-wood, 3-wood, 4-wood, 5-wood, 7-wood, and 9-wood. The higher the number, the more loft the club has, and the more loft, the higher and shorter the ball should travel when hit properly.

It is important to keep head covers on both your driver and your fairway woods to prevent their longer shafts from being damaged while in your bag.

## IRONS AND HYBRIDS

Irons have a completely different shape and size of clubhead than woods and drivers do. They are numbered in an ascending order (from 1 to 9) that corresponds to the amount of loft the clubface has, and each iron comes in different lengths. The more loft an iron has, the shorter your shot should travel.

Iron clubheads come in a variety of types, including:

- **Forged:** A block of solid metal is shaved down to form this club. The detailed process used usually makes forged irons the most expensive type.

- **Cast:** Metal is poured into a mold to make this club, allowing a wider range of shapes to be used.

- **Offset:** The term *offset* describes the point at which the shaft joins the clubhead: The leading edge of this club is slightly behind the hosel. Offset irons are highly recommended for beginners since they help keep the hands in proper position at impact.

- **Cavity-back:** This type of iron has a space carved out just behind the clubface, enabling more perimeter weighting around the edge of the club. This extra weighting makes the iron more forgiving of off-center hits by creating a larger sweet spot.

A starter set of irons should be offset with a cavity back and a low center of gravity. The offset design of the shaft will help you visually when aiming the club as well as keep your hands ahead of the ball. The cavity-back design and low center of gravity will make the ball fly higher if struck properly.

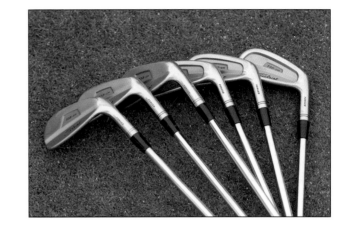

In recent years, an increasing number of professional and amateur golfers are replacing the 3-iron and 4-iron with a new type of club called a *hybrid.* Hybrid clubs blend a wood and an iron and help players get the ball up into the air more effectively than the low-numbered irons. Because hybrids have longer shafts than irons do, you can generate more swing speed and more distance. A selection of hybrids, which vary by degree of loft, are available, although each manufacturer labels its products differently—unlike irons, which are always identified by the same numbers. Hybrids can also be used for approach shots around the green (see Chapter 6). When purchasing a new set of clubs, we recommend that you substitute hybrids, which can be purchased separately, for the lower irons.

**CONTINUED ON NEXT PAGE**

# Clubs
## (continued)

## WEDGES

Wedges are the clubs with the highest amount of loft on the clubface. You use them for approach shots to the green, whether you are in the fairway, rough, or sand. Because of their loft, these clubs add height to a shot, as well as impart spin on the ball because of the angle at which the clubface strikes the ball.

Many types are available, including the pitching wedge, gap wedge, sand wedge, and lob wedge, in ascending order of loft on the clubface. As with woods, the degree of loft determines just how high in the air the ball will go: The greater the degree of loft, the higher the ball goes if struck properly. A starter set of golf clubs usually includes a pitching wedge and a sand wedge. A standard pitching wedge has a loft of 48 degrees, while a standard sand wedge comes with a 54- to 57-degree loft. As your ability to control the distance of your shots improves, consider purchasing additional wedges with different lofts (i.e., 52, 56, 58, and 60 degrees) that can be used for particular yardages.

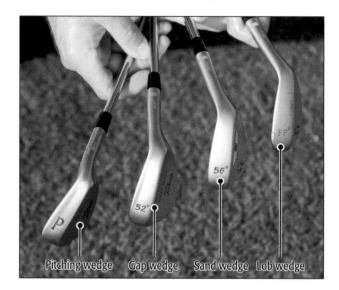

Pitching wedge    Gap wedge    Sand wedge    Lob wedge

## PUTTERS

The object of the game of golf is to get the ball into the hole, and the club that almost always does that is the putter. This club comes in many different shapes and sizes. The most important factor is what you feel most comfortable using.

From bottom to top:

- **Scotty Cameron Detour:** This type of putter contains visual elements (such as a curving extension behind the clubface) to promote a certain type of swing path (inside going back, square at impact, and inside going through).

- **Blade:** This standard putter type features a very small "sweet spot" on the clubface, making it hard for beginners to use successfully.

- **Futura:** Large mallet-type putters like this one help distribute weight behind the clubface, which can help you balance the club through the putter stroke.

- **Classic:** This type of putter offers a sightline right behind the clubface and is weighted on the heel and toe to help promote a smooth, balanced stroke.

- **Odyssey Two Ball:** This type of putter features white circles shaped like golf balls directly behind the clubface to help you align the putt visually.

Whatever type you choose, keep a head cover on your putter to keep it from being damaged while in your bag.

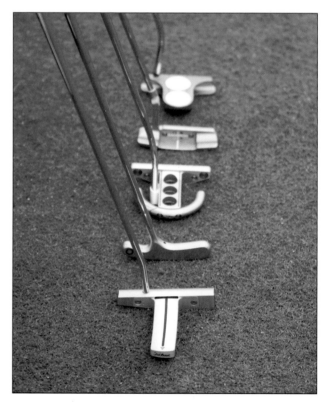

A golf club is made up of several individual components that are brought together as one during the club-making process. The three main parts are the *shaft* (which can be made of either steel or a lighter material called graphite), the *clubhead* (the shape and size of which depends on the type of club being made), and the *grip* (which is attached to the shaft so you can hold the club properly).

## Driver and Iron Parts

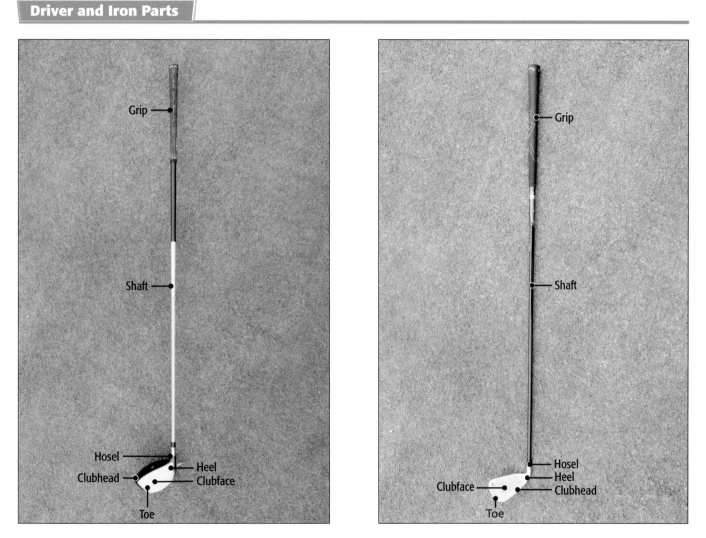

**CONTINUED ON NEXT PAGE**

## GRIP

The grip is your physical connection to each club. Different materials are used in grips, but all are designed to enable you to maintain your hold on the club during your swing. Grips do wear out over time, so it's important to have them replaced as needed.

## SHAFT

Shafts are made primarily out of steel or graphite. Either material can be used in the shaft of any club, but steel is usually used for irons and wedges, while graphite, which is lighter, is found mostly in drivers and woods to promote higher swing speeds.

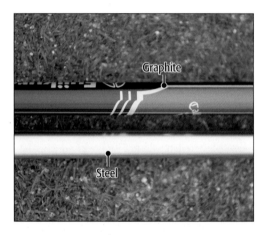

## HOSEL AND CLUBFACE

The clubface is the part of the club that strikes the ball. While your goal is always to hit the ball with the center, or "sweet spot," of the clubface, you may hit the ball off the *heel,* which is the end closest to the shaft, or the *toe,* which is the end farthest from the shaft.

The *hosel* is where the shaft connects to the clubhead. A ball struck with this portion of the club is likely to go off in a sideways direction.

The official limit on the number of clubs you can carry in your bag during a competitive round is 14, but beginners should try out as many varieties of clubs as possible before purchasing a set. You want to find clubs that feel comfortable and work with your natural tendencies.

## Buying Your First Set of Clubs

Golf clubs are sold at sporting goods stores, specialized golf equipment stores, and pro shops at golf courses. Irons and woods are usually sold separately in sets, while hybrids, putters, and wedges can be bought individually. A basic beginner set usually includes a driver, two woods (usually a 3-wood and a 5-wood), irons 3 through 9, a pitching wedge, and a putter. As your playing experience grows, you will have a large variety of club and shaft types to choose from to suit your individual game.

With all the choices available to you, buying a set of golf clubs can be an intimidating experience, especially since rows and rows of clubs and starter sets line the aisles of most golf equipment stores. As with any other purchase, you need to do some research. Read the equipment testing guides published annually by the major golf magazines. Hit balls using a variety of clubs at a golf equipment store, or try out the demo clubs that may be available at driving ranges. Visit the websites of equipment manufacturers for information about their products. Many golf clubs are now being sold on eBay, which can give you some perspective on price ranges. The more details you have, the better decisions you can make.

The best option, however, is to contact a PGA or LPGA professional both for advice and to arrange a club-fitting session. Your height and build affect the type and length of club that best suits you. During a fitting session, a professional measures your body in relation to a golf club and analyzes your swing (usually on video) to gauge your swing speed and typical ball flight. This information enables the professional to recommend the appropriate length, shaft type, and lie angle of clubs, including putters, for you.

*CONTINUED ON NEXT PAGE*

## CLUB DISTANCE CHART

The following table gives suggested average distances for each club. How far *you* hit the ball depends on many factors—how hard you swing, how the clubface meets the ball at impact, weather and course conditions, etc.—but these distances give you a general idea of how far each club can hit a ball on average.

| Club Distance Chart | | |
| --- | --- | --- |
| *Club* | *Men's Average Distance* | *Women's Average Distance* |
| Driver | 225+ yards | 180+ yards |
| 3-wood | 210 yards | 170 yards |
| 5-wood | 190 yards | 160 yards |
| 7-wood | — | 150 yards |
| 9-wood | — | 140 yards |
| 3-hybrid | 180 yards | — |
| 4-iron/4-hybrid | 170 yards | 135 yards |
| 5-iron/5-hybrid | 160 yards | 125 yards |
| 6-iron | 150 yards | 110 yards |
| 7-iron | 140 yards | 100 yards |
| 8-iron | 125 yards | 90 yards |
| 9-iron | 115 yards | 80 yards |
| Pitching wedge | 95 yards | 70 yards |
| Sand wedge | 75 yards | 50 yards |
| Lob wedge | 50 yards | — |

With top-of-the-line golf clubs in your bag, you can take an enjoyable walk around the course, but you can't play golf. To do that, you need to purchase golf balls and tees on which to place them.

## BALLS

There are almost as many brands of golf balls to choose from as there are golf clubs. You can buy them in sleeves (or boxes) of three, or by the dozen. The basic types are:

- **Hard:** Built for more distance with a harder feel, this is the cheaper of the two types.

- **Soft:** Considered a "softer" ball because of the materials used in it, this type enables golfers to impart more spin during shots.

The difference between the two types of golf balls is less important to beginners than it is to more advanced players. You can try both types to see which plays better for you, but in general, beginners should consider buying the harder balls. Their lower spin rate means less side spin and likely more accuracy while you are learning the game.

## TEES

Even golf tees vary in size, shape, and color. You will probably use a long tee when teeing off with a driver to ensure that the ball sits up high. Shorter tees are used for iron, hybrid, and wedge shots, when you want the ball to be lower to the ground. Other tees, such as the brush tee pictured here, are available in various materials or designs to promote improved contact between the clubface and the ball.

**Note:** *If you play in a competition, check with the rules official about the regulations regarding tees. Tees other than the standard short and long ones may not be allowed.*

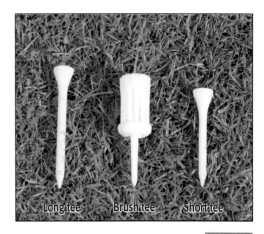

Long tee    Brush tee    Short tee

# Carrying Your Clubs: Golf Bags and Carts

## BAG

The design of golf bags has advanced almost as quickly as that of golf clubs in the past decade. While professionals use large leather bags, much lighter options are available for everyday golfers.

Carry bags, designed for golfers who walk rather than ride a cart, have legs that stand the cart up while you take a shot. These bags also have double straps that enable you to carry the bag across both of your shoulders like a backpack.

## CARTS

Most courses offer carts for golfers to ride in. You can secure your golf bags in the rear of these mini-cars, affix your scorecard to the steering wheel, keep extra balls and tees in slots on the dashboard, and stow jackets and additional clothes in a basket behind the seat. Some carts provide room for refreshments, and some include a Global Positioning System (GPS), which shows images of each hole and informs you of the yardage for each shot.

For golfers who want to walk while playing but don't want to carry their bags, there are pull carts. These carts hold your golf bag and come equipped with wheels that enable you to pull the clubs along with you as you play.

## CLOTHING

Most public courses require that golfers wear only appropriate types of clothing at their facilities. Call it a business casual look: usually a collared shirt and pants or shorts. Inappropriate clothing almost always includes jeans and T-shirts.

All private clubs have strict dress codes; some prohibit golfers from wearing shorts even on the hottest days. Always call the club ahead of time to ask about the dress code.

Certain types of clothing materials help block wind and rain and keep you dry. If you know you will be playing frequently in these conditions, a rain suit (jacket, pants, and a hat) is a good investment.

## SHOES AND GLOVE

Purchase shoes designed specifically for golf. In the past, golf shoes featured metal spikes on the soles to help balance the golfer during the swing. These days, metal has been replaced by Softspikes, which provide stability without digging as deep into the ground. Shoes come in a variety of styles and colors.

Wearing a glove while playing golf is a personal choice. Some golfers never wear one, while others always do. Most wear a glove on the hand that grips the club first: the left hand for righties, the right hand for lefties. Gloves come in many sizes, and fit is the most important consideration in choosing one. Some gloves also contain a ball marker that snaps on and off.

# Other Essentials and Nice-to-Have Gadgets

Golfers love gadgets. Plenty of them promise better swings, more distance, and lower scores. Few of them replace good lessons and practice, but there are some useful gadgets that you should have.

There's a reason your bag has so many compartments—you'll need space for various items, especially if you're playing in less-than-ideal weather. Some—like a ball marker and a divot repair tool—are used on every hole, while others, like a towel, can be used after every shot. All of them are worth the investment—they will benefit you and the courses you play.

Use a ball marker on the putting surface (the green) to identify the position of your ball when it is in the way of someone else's putt, or when you want to pick up your ball to clean it off. You must mark that spot on the green if you're going to touch the ball. Ball markers are usually small and round (between the size of a dime and a nickel, which also can be used as ball markers) and often have a logo on them.

Use a divot repair tool on the green when your ball has made an indentation upon landing. The tool has two prongs that you insert into the ground around the divot to help repair the mark left by the ball's impact. Always repair your own divots and any others you happen to see on the green.

A club brush helps clean dirt and grass from the clubface. A clean clubface is important because dirt and grass can affect the amount of spin on the ball after it's struck. Always keep your clubfaces as clean as possible.

Having a towel and an umbrella in your golf bag is important in both poor and fair weather. An umbrella will keep you and your clubs dry during rain, while you can use a towel to dry the grips of your clubs. You can also use a towel to keep your golf clubs clean no matter what the weather. You should clean your clubs after every round to help reduce wear and tear.

A range finder is a device that calculates shot distance for you. By focusing on a target (usually the top of the flagstick on the green), the device calculates the exact yardage between that point and your ball. If you're playing in a competition, be sure to check whether the use of range finders is allowed during play.

If you're having a tough time on a particular hole, keeping track of how many shots you've taken can be a challenge. Instead of marking down that number on a piece of paper that can easily get lost while you progress from shot to shot, consider a bead counter that you can adjust after each stroke—hopefully to keep track of the fewest number of strokes possible!

# chapter 3

# Getting Set: Your Grip and Stance

Even the most expensive set of golf clubs in the world won't help your game unless you have the proper grip. How to hold the club is the single most important lesson you may ever learn, because your grip will affect both the power and accuracy of your shots. This chapter discusses the steps to making a proper grip and the different types of grips you can use, as well as the proper stance and alignment you should assume to begin your swing.

Establishing a good grip is essential to making a sound swing. Building a proper grip is a two-step process involving the placement of your left hand and then the placement of your right hand on the club (or the opposite sequence for left-handers).

Consistent grip pressure is needed throughout the swing. A poor grip can't keep hold of two tees (as in the photo), especially if there is too much space between the right thumb and forefinger. That leads to changing the grip pressure during the swing or overswinging, since the shaft will drop in your hands at the top of the backswing.

## Take the Club with Your Left Hand

**1** Take hold of the club with your left hand. The club should touch the two points indicated by the Xs, with your left index finger and the opposite side of your palm's heel pad touching the grip.

*Note: Assuming the proper grip with your left hand enables you to hold the club in the air simply by curling your left index finger around the club.*

**2** Close your left hand on the club. Look for your thumb and index finger to form a V-shape. The bottom of this V should point toward your right shoulder.

**3** Maintaining this grip with your left hand, lift the club straight up in the air. In a standard (or neutral) grip, you should see two knuckles on the left side of the shaft, and your thumb should rest on the right side of center on the shaft.

## Add Your Right Hand

With your left hand on the club, place your right hand directly below it, resting naturally on the club. The exact placement of the right hand's fingers will depend on the type of grip you choose (see pages 45–46 for the different grip types).

With both hands on the club, the center of your right palm will rest directly on top of your left thumb. Your left thumb should rest against the lifeline of your right palm. Your right index finger should be separated from your middle finger and curved around the grip as if you were pulling the trigger on a gun.

The thumb and forefinger of each hand should form a V-shape. Your best chance of hitting the ball straight is to ensure that the bottom of each V is pointing toward your right shoulder. If the Vs are facing right of that point, your clubface will tend to be closed at impact, and your shot will go low and left. If they are facing left of your right shoulder, your clubface will tend to be open at impact, and the ball will go right.

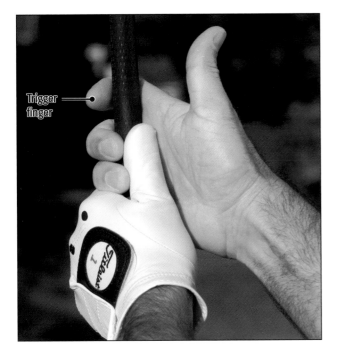

Trigger finger

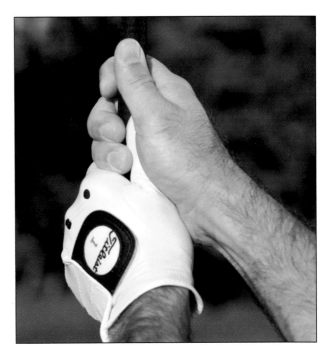

# Find the Right Grip Pressure

The amount of pressure you exert with your grip is very important because it affects your ability to make a good golf swing. Holding the club too tightly will tense your arm muscles and limit your club speed. Holding the club too loosely means that you lose control of the clubhead and your accuracy suffers. A good grip pressure is the same pressure you would use when holding a child's hand.

The grip pressure of your left hand comes mainly from the middle, ring, and pinky fingers. On your right hand, the index finger, middle finger, and thumb supply the pressure.

## Match Your Grip Pressure to Your Shot

For the most part, you should use a steady grip pressure throughout the swing. However, different situations call for different levels of pressure. For example, hitting a ball out of deep, heavy grass requires a firmer grip than hitting a ball off the fairway. The following table gives you some guidelines for adjusting your grip pressure to the shot you're facing, with 1 representing the loosest grip and 10 representing the tightest grip.

| Situation | Grip Pressure |
| --- | --- |
| High, soft shot | 3 |
| Fairway shot | 6 |
| Shot out of heavy rough | 8 |

## TIP

After you have gripped a club, hold it straight out in front of you and ask someone to try to pull it out of your hands. If your grip pressure is too loose, they will be able to yank it away easily. If they can't move the club at all, your grip pressure is too tight. If the club moves slightly forward in your hands but does not come completely out, then your grip pressure is just right.

Golfers use multiple types of grips. Choose the one that feels the most comfortable to you.

## OVERLAPPING

In the overlapping grip, the pinky of your right hand rests on top of the space between the index and middle fingers of your left hand. We recommend this grip because it promotes a feeling of connection between the hands and the club.

## INTERLOCKING

In the interlocking grip, the pinky of your right hand and the index finger of your left hand are interlaced. Golfers with small fingers should consider the interlocking grip for a better hold on the club.

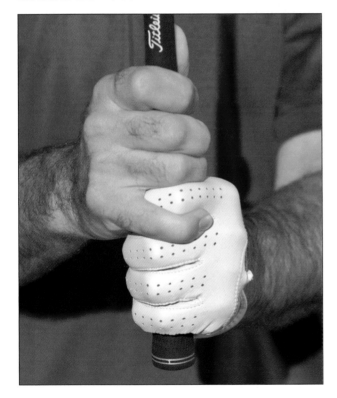

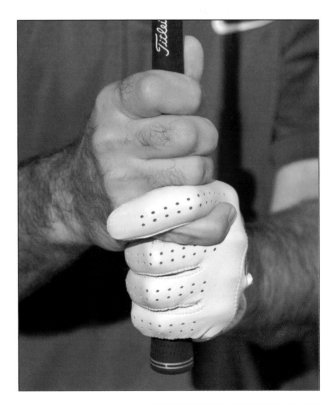

**CONTINUED ON NEXT PAGE**

## BASEBALL

With the baseball grip, also known as the ten-finger grip, all ten of your fingers touch the club, and your right thumb is below your left thumb.

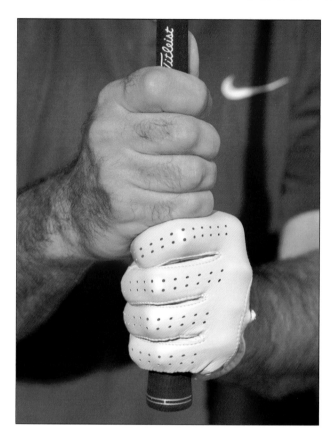

### TIP

Women tend to have smaller hands and fingers, which can make gripping the club a bit more difficult. First, make sure that you get the smallest grips available for your clubs. Then try the baseball grip, where all ten fingers are on the club. This grip should feel more comfortable and secure to you than trying to interlock or overlap your pinky finger.

Within each of the three grip types are different hand positions that affect the position of the clubface when it hits the ball. A neutral grip is ideal for all shots and most golfers. As your skills improve, you can begin to experiment with strong and weak grips to hit draw shots and fade shots, respectively.

## WEAK

A weak grip describes the position of your hands on the club when you can see less than two knuckles on your left hand and one or two on your right hand. In this position, the Vs formed by your hands point toward your left shoulder.

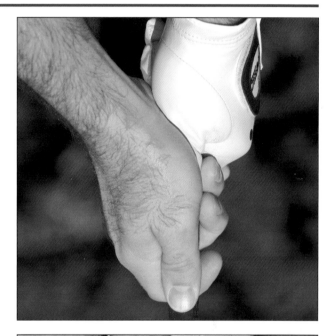

## STRONG

With a strong grip, you see three knuckles on your left hand and one or none on your right. In this position, the Vs formed by your hands point toward the outside of your right shoulder.

*CONTINUED ON NEXT PAGE*

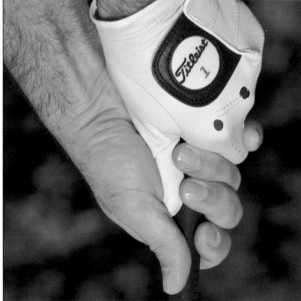

## NEUTRAL

With a neutral grip, you can see one or two knuckles on your left hand and one knuckle on your right hand. In this position, the Vs formed by your hands point toward your right shoulder.

## TIP

Many beginners tend to hit the ball to the right. A short-term solution to that problem is to create a stronger grip by rotating your left hand to the right after you place it on the club. When you do so, you will see two to three knuckles on your left hand and one knuckle on your right hand. Keep in mind, though, that strengthening your grip can lead to the opposite problem: shots that pull to the left. See Chapter 10 for drills that will help you straighten things out.

Once you have established your grip, you need to stand in the proper position. In order to finish your swing in balance, you must begin your swing in balance. If you don't, your body will try to rebalance itself during the swing, throwing weight shift and clubhead position out of whack. A balanced stance is also easier to repeat and involves less unnecessary motion than an unbalanced swing.

## Find the Proper Stance

The stance you take will be almost identical for every full-swing golf shot, which is why establishing a comfortable position that you can repeat over and over is important. In certain situations, such as when chipping, hitting bunker shots, or putting, you will alter your stance, but in general you should:

- Bend forward from the hips.
- Flex your knees slightly.
- Keep your back straight, without any arch.
- Tilt your spine slightly to the right to raise your left shoulder above your right shoulder.
- Let your hands hang directly underneath your shoulders.
- Point the grip end of the club between your belly button and belt buckle.
- Keep your feet parallel to one another unless you are setting up to hit a draw or fade (see page 53).
- Distribute your weight evenly between your feet.
- Keep your weight between your toes and heels—think of the area underneath your shoelaces.

When you have achieved the proper stance, you should feel like you are standing on the edge of a pool getting ready to dive into the water.

***CONTINUED ON NEXT PAGE***

Here are two examples of what you should *not* be doing in your stance:

- Reaching out to the ball with your arms overextended. Overextending your arms puts most of your weight over your toes, leading to an unbalanced swing.

- Standing too upright and rigid without any knee flex. This creates tension that prevents your shoulders from making a good turn. It also creates a downswing that is far too steep, which can cause you to top the ball (hit the top of the ball) or hit a chunked shot (hit the ground behind the ball, sending a chunk of turf flying farther than the ball).

While your stance remains essentially the same for most swings, the position of the ball within your stance will change depending on the club you are using.

## Tips for Positioning the Ball

The distance between you and the ball is determined by the length of the club you are using, as shown at left. Your arms should hang naturally from your shoulders, without you having to reach out toward the ball.

The longer the club you are using, the more toward the front of your stance you should position the ball, as shown at right. The ball ideally should be positioned at the point where your swing bottoms out. The longer the club, the farther forward in your stance that point will be.

Follow these general guidelines when positioning the ball between your feet:

- **Driver and woods:** Position the ball forward in your stance, off the inside of your left heel.
- **Irons and hybrids:** Position the ball nearer to the center of your stance.
- **Wedges:** Position the ball slightly right of center.

# Align Your Shot

The way you aim at your target and line up to hit the ball is as important as the swing you make. Altering your stance, or repositioning your feet, will directly affect the path the ball takes after leaving the clubface.

## Take Aim

Before every shot, you must select a target. It could be the flagstick, a particular area of the green, or a spot on the fairway. As you place your club behind the ball, make sure that the clubface is pointed at your target, and then take your stance. Imagine that you're standing on railroad tracks, your feet and body on one rail, the ball and clubhead on the other.

While your clubface is aimed at the target, your shoulders, hips, and feet should naturally point just left of the target. If your feet are pointing directly at the target, your ball and clubface are pointed to the right of it. Most golfers aim too far to the right and then compensate by swinging their arms too far to the left, usually creating a shot that pulls to the left.

## DRAW SHOTS

When the ball gradually moves from right to left in the air after being hit, the shot is called a *draw*. To hit this shot, you must angle your feet so that your line points to the right of the target. This stance will produce an inside-out swing that helps impart spin on the ball that will make it curve to the left.

## FADE SHOTS

When the ball gradually moves from left to right in the air after being hit, the shot is called a *fade*. To hit this shot, you must angle your feet so that your line points to the left of the target. This stance will produce an outside-in swing that helps impart spin on the ball that will make it curve to the right.

**FAQ**

**Why would I want to hit a draw or fade on purpose?**

As your skills improve, so too will your ability to shape the flight path of your ball—the curve to the right or left. Suppose your ball comes to rest behind a tree in the fairway. If the pin is on the far right side of the green, then you want to hit a fade that curves around the tree from left to right and rolls toward the hole. If the pin is on the far left side of the green, then you want hit a draw from right to left toward the hole.

Just as your stance affects the direction of the ball, so does the position of the clubface when it strikes the ball. A square clubface will likely produce a straight shot.

It's important to focus on lining the leading edge of the iron up to the ball so that it is perpendicular to your target line. Many golfers try to line up the top part of the iron and end up with a closed clubface, as shown in the bottom photo on this page.

An open clubface will likely produce a fade or slice shot that curves to the right.

A closed clubface will likely produce a draw or hook shot that curves to the left.

# 4

# The Iron Swing

It don't mean a thing if you ain't got that swing. This chapter discusses the makeup of a basic golf swing: the address, backswing, downswing, and finish. While some specific clubs (a sand wedge, for example) and some particular situations (such as hitting out of deep rough or a bunker) require a specific type of swing, these basics will help you hit the majority of the iron shots you will face on the course.

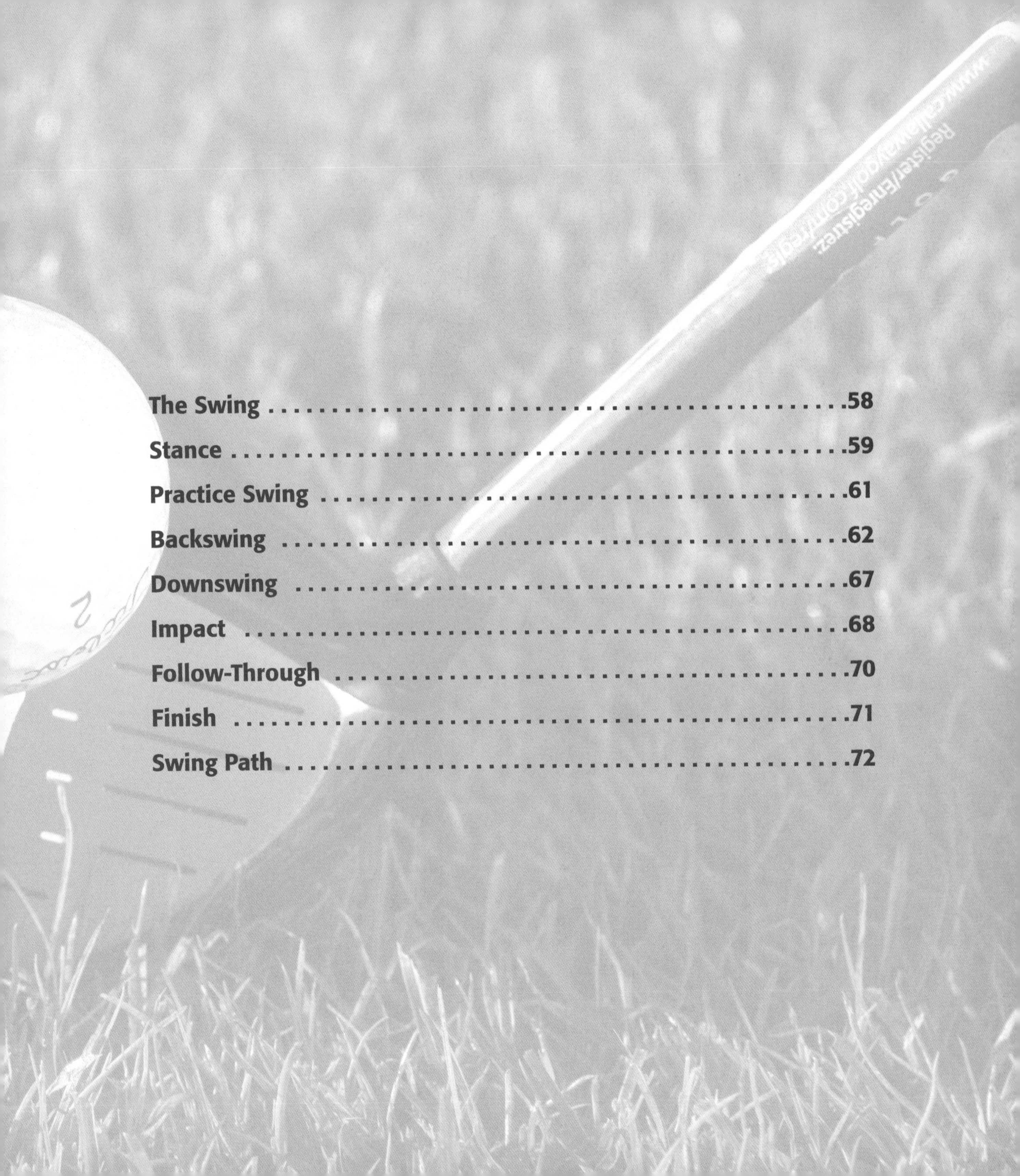

# The Swing

For many people, the golf swing is a race to see how fast they can make the club go up and then down to hit the ball. Rarely does anything good come of that approach. Instead, the golf swing—for beginners and experienced golfers alike—should be about balance and tempo. You will make stronger and perhaps faster swings as you gain experience, but right now the priority is to learn how to swing properly and efficiently. And remember that no two swings are alike—the shape and size of your body, plus your flexibility, will determine what your swing looks like.

Irons require a blend of accuracy and power. Eventually, these are the clubs you will need to be hitting onto greens to lower your score. If you can drive, pitch, and putt well, you will likely play a good round of golf. But to get even better, you will need to hit shots to greens that get you closer and closer to the pin as your experience grows. That means getting used to your 6-iron through 9-iron via practice, which will create the consistency needed to score well.

Deciding which club to use is tough for beginners. Over time, you will learn how far you can hit each club. If you're just beginning to play, go with a more lofted one to help you get the ball up into the air more easily.

While you are developing your swing, you may be thinking of 100 different things: Where's my elbow? Is my grip right? Did I shift my weight correctly? The list of questions can be endless. Instead, try to concentrate on one particular element each time you play. Focus on your grip for an entire round, and commit to putting the correct grip on the club even if you don't hit shots well. If you feel you need another round to get that aspect correct, do it instead of moving on to another element of the swing. You can focus on your backswing in another round, or on your follow-through another time. You can't practice every single element of the swing at once. Think of it like building a house—you can't put the roof on until you have created a strong foundation, piece by piece.

# Stance

Every good swing begins with the proper stance. When using an iron, position the ball between your left heel and the center point of your stance. Remember that as your clubs get longer (for example, a 5-iron is longer than a 7-iron, which in turn is longer than a 9-iron), the position of the ball within your stance changes. The longer the club, the more forward the ball should be in your stance.

## Ball Position

For a 4-iron or an equivalent hybrid club, position the ball a few inches inside your front heel.

For a 5-iron, 6-iron, or 7-iron, position the ball roughly an inch left of center, as shown here.

For an 8-iron or 9-iron, position the ball in the center of your stance, as shown here.

For a wedge, position the ball slightly behind center.

*CONTINUED ON NEXT PAGE*

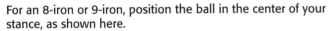

## Balance and Posture

The width of your stance is affected in a similar way—the longer the club, the wider the stance. Keep in mind that your heels should not go outside of your shoulders, nor should they be narrower than hip width apart.

The more forward the ball is in your stance, the more your shoulders will tilt naturally from left to right. You should feel slightly more than half of your weight toward your right leg. As the ball moves from the front of your stance to the center, your shoulders become more level, and your weight should become more equally balanced on both legs. Your head should be just behind the ball, with your hands just ahead of the ball.

Head slightly behind ball

Shoulders tilted left to right

Hands ahead of the ball

Weight balanced equally between feet

Shaft leaning forward

Feet no wider than shoulder width apart

## TIP

Posture is very important during every swing. You must allow your shoulders to turn properly; any imbalance in your posture (such as standing stiffly or slouching) prevents that rotation from occurring. Many golfers find other ways to make a bigger swing—allowing the left arm to break down at the top of the backswing, turning the head away from the ball, straightening the right knee, over-rotating the hips, or swaying with the whole body—but those short-term solutions are rarely effective in the long run. For more information, refer to Chapter 3.

Always take one practice swing before playing an iron shot to establish your swing tempo and visualize the shot you want to hit.

Make sure that you hit the ground when taking a practice swing—doing so will help you get the feel of the turf and reinforce the idea that you want to take a divot. Don't be afraid to hit the ground; divots are okay, and you should make one whenever the ball is on the ground (except when it's on the green). Just remember to fix your divot, either by placing the turf back in the divot or by spreading sand (usually provided in your golf cart) on the spot.

Don't panic if you miss the ground during that practice swing, though. You don't want to take multiple practice swings, since that would slow down the pace of play. Just set up to the ball, look at the target, and then take your swing. Whatever your goal is—whether it's simply advancing the ball or hitting the ball onto the green—commit your thoughts to that goal during the swing.

# Backswing

The purpose of the backswing is to create leverage that will build power. You turn your shoulders, your arms go up and around your body, and the club is lifted into the air. The simpler the backswing, the easier it will be to repeat consistently. And a good backswing only enhances your chances of making a good downswing. If your backswing goes off the correct path, you will have to recover on the downswing, forcing you to rely too much on timing.

## First Move of Backswing

After getting into your stance, take one more look at your target before you start your swing. As you begin the backswing, your hands, arms, and shoulders and the clubhead should be turning back and inside away from the ball, with your wrists beginning to hinge.

## Halfway Back

Continue to swing the club farther back and allow your wrists to hinge. The club should be at a 45-degree angle to your left arm, and your weight slowly moving into your right heel. If there were water in the shaft of the club, water would be pouring out of the grip end at this point in the swing.

If the club is parallel to the ground here, you have not hinged your wrists enough. If you don't create this hinge, it will be difficult to generate any power.

### TIP

To feel a proper wrist hinge, grip a club and hold straight out in front of you. Then point the club straight up in the air in front of you (your thumbs should be pointing up). You've just hinged your wrists. An improper hinge makes your wrists point to the left or to the right.

*CONTINUED ON NEXT PAGE*

## Top of Backswing

At the top of your backswing, the shaft of the club should be roughly parallel to the ground. Your ability to reach that position depends on your range of motion: More flexible golfers can get the shaft parallel to the ground, while less flexible golfers might not be able to reach parallel—and that's okay.

If you can see the club out of the corner of your left eye at this point, then you're overswinging. You may see PGA Tour pros like John Daly and Phil Mickelson bring their clubs this far back, but they are tremendously skilled golfers whose rhythm is finely tuned from hitting thousands of balls. As a beginner, it's far more important for you to build a repeatable swing within your own abilities than it is to imitate the swing of a professional golfer.

Ideally, your left arm at this point should be as long and straight as it was at address. Your left shoulder should be behind the ball to make a full turn and pointed downward, and the club should be pointing in the general direction of the target. Your hips will have turned approximately 45 degrees, and your right knee will be flexed. Most of your weight should be toward the inside of your right heel.

The clubface should be square at the top of the backswing.

If the clubface is closed, as shown here, the ball will likely move toward the left after you hit it. Golfers compensate for this problem by swinging their arms and the club to the right of the target, but doing so leads to pushes and hooks.

If the clubface is open, as shown here, the ball will likely move toward the right after being struck. Golfers try to compensate for this problem by swinging their arms and the club to the left of the target, but doing so leads to pulls and slices.

**CONTINUED ON NEXT PAGE**

Your left wrist should be flat, while your left forearm and hand should be in line at the top of the backswing. Any bend between the left wrist and forearm means that the clubface will be either opening or closing at impact. Do you feel like you could put a ruler flat against the back of your left hand and your forearm? That's the feeling you're trying to achieve here.

Your right elbow should be bent and pointing down at the ground if your body is flexible enough to reach that position; if not, it will likely point more behind your body. Though not recommended, this "flying right elbow" has worked for a number of great golfers, including Jack Nicklaus.

There should also be a gap between the right elbow and your body. If your elbow is pinned against your ribcage, then you have to compensate in some way on the downswing to get it away from your body and create that space. If you don't, your swing will lack power, you will make poor contact with the ball, and the clubhead will bottom out much too soon during the swing, resulting in fat or possibly topped shots.

Grip

Left forearm and hand in line

Right elbow bent and away from body

## TIP

If you're struggling with iron shots, try using only your favorite club for all shots (except for sand shots and putts) on a few holes to re-establish your comfort level. Doing so will also help you get creative by forcing you to play different shots—it might even be fun!

# Downswing

Remember the power you were trying to build with your backswing? The downswing—where the club moves back toward the ball—is where that power is unleashed. In fact, it is even more important to execute the downswing properly, since this is the portion of the swing that leads directly to impact with the ball.

As you begin your downswing, your weight should start moving toward your left side. Your hips will rotate to the left, turning your belly button toward the target. Your shoulders and arms will follow.

As the club gets closer to impact, the grip end should be pointing in the direction of the ball.

If a straight line were drawn at waist level, your hands and the grip end of the club would be below it, while the clubhead would still be above it.

# Impact

At impact, your head should be behind the club. Your left arm, your left shoulder, and the club should form almost a straight line coming up from the ball. The inside of your right foot should still be on the ground, and your hips and belt buckle should be rotating toward the target. Most of your weight should be on your left leg at this point.

## TIP

You can see evidence of where the ball makes contact with the club by placing tape on the clubface. Special tape designed for this purpose is available from most club fitters. (You can also sprinkle the clubface with baby powder to get the same effect.) The mark left by the ball enables you to see the exact point of impact. Practice range balls usually leave a mark on the clubface, too, so it can be helpful to look at your club after a swing to notice the impact point (heel, center, or toe).

If you're hitting shots off the toe or heel, go back to hitting partial shots (three-quarter swings) during your practice session. Doing so will help you find the center of the clubface and remind you what solid contact feels like.

The correct impact feels solid and almost effortless, with no twisting of the club or vibration running up the shaft into your hands. It's more important to make solid contact in the center of the clubface than to attempt to achieve maximum power. You will attain maximum distance only after you learn to strike the ball with the center of the clubface. Ask your golf professional for a few pieces of impact tape to learn where you're making contact with the ball.

Most golfers complain that they feel the club move in their hands during a poor swing. What they are feeling are vibrations caused by the ball when it hits the inside (heel) of the clubface...

...or the outside (toe) of the clubface.

# Follow-Through

Just after impact, the club should be pointing toward the target. Your right heel will come up off the ground, and your left leg will be fully extended. Your right wrist will be closer to the target than your left wrist.

**TIP**

Halfway through a proper follow-through, your right hand will be hip high. It should be positioned as if you were going to shake someone's hand right in front of you.

All your weight should be over your left heel at the finish. Your right shoulder should be lower than your left, just as when you began the swing. The shaft of the club should be right behind your neck. Your right heel will be up in the air, with all spikes showing and only the toes touching the ground, and your belt buckle should point toward the target. (That will depend on your flexibility, though: The belt buckle could be more to the left for those with a greater range of motion, or more to the right for those who are less flexible. Either way is generally okay.)

A balanced finish is critical to a good swing. Without balance, you won't be able to repeat the swing consistently. The position may be uncomfortable when you're just beginning to play, but your body will get used to supporting your weight in that position with practice.

# Swing Path

The path along which you swing the club is the main influence on the direction your ball starts flying after impact. Called the *swing path*, it refers to the direction of the clubhead as it moves through the swing. Because you move the golf club up and around your body during a swing, it is never taken back and then forward on a purely straight line—rather, it should move along an arc. Any curvature of the ball that happens after the initial moment when it leaves the clubface will be a result of the position of the clubface at impact.

## Proper Path

In the best possible swing, the clubhead moves on an inside-square-inside path; that means that during the downswing, the clubhead moves along the inside of the target line, returns to impact (square to the ball) on the target line, and then, after the ball is struck, moves to the inside again. This natural swing path enables your body to serve as the axis of what we hope will be a repetitive motion.

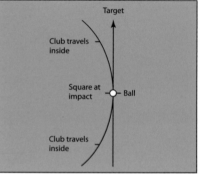

During this swing path, if the clubface is square at impact, the ball should move directly toward your target. If the clubface is open at impact, the ball will curve to the right; if it's closed, the ball will curve left.

# chapter 4

## Outside-Inside Path

In this swing path, the club-head travels outside of the target line during the down-swing so that at impact you are hitting across the ball to the left and then moving the clubhead sharply inside the target line. This path can result in everything from a hook to a dramatic slice, depending on the position of the clubface at impact. If it's open, it could create a massive slice back toward the target line; if closed, a dramatic hook that starts left and contin-ues farther left could result. If the clubface is square at impact, you will likely hit a pull shot that heads left.

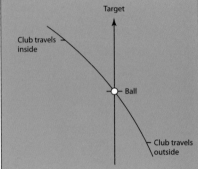

## Inside-Outside Path

In this swing path, the club-head travels back to impact from too far inside the tar-get line; then, at impact, it continues farther out and well right of the target line. If the clubface is open at impact, the ball will start right of the target line and curve farther in that direc-tion; if closed, the ball will start right and then curve back to the left toward the target line in a hook; and if square, the ball will be pushed straight to the right.

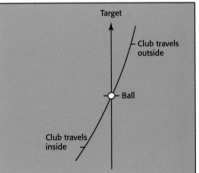

# 5

# Driving

There may be no better feeling than standing on the tee with the biggest club in your hand, hitting a perfect drive, and watching it soar down the fairway. To do so, you need to have certain fundamentals in place. This chapter describes the process of using your driver (and some alternative clubs) on the tee: using the tee box to your advantage, teeing the ball up correctly, and making a proper swing. We also include some practice drills to help you get the most from your tee shots.

Everyone wants to hit gigantic drives and to be known as the longest hitter in the group. Most people think that swinging hard and fast will generate big hits that will leave your playing partners in awe of your power and strength. The reality of this approach is that you wind up hitting shots deep—but into the woods. Your goal for driving should be square, solid contact, which leads to a good blend of accuracy and distance. You must make a solid, balanced swing and let the club do the work.

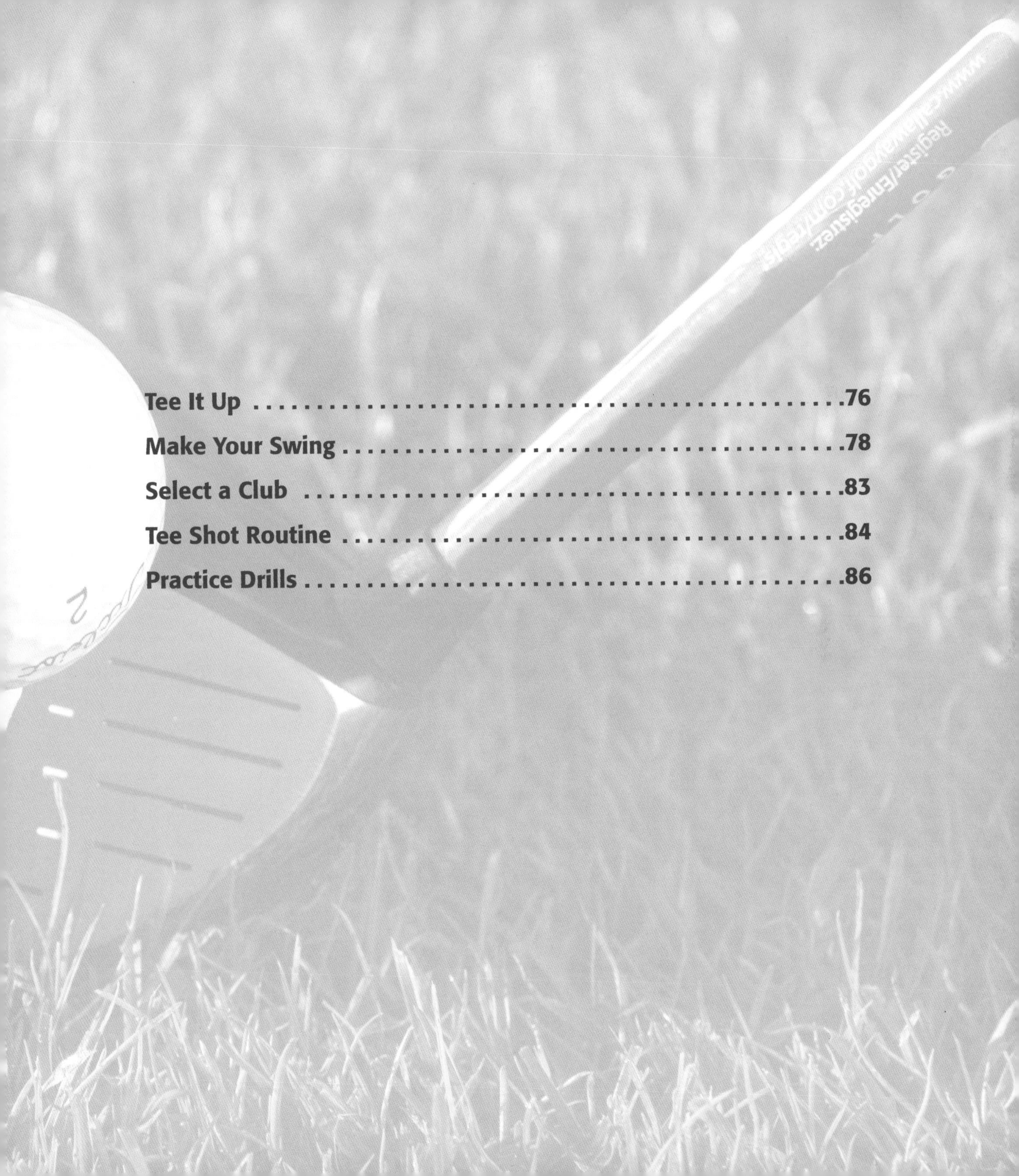

# Tee It Up

Driving the ball successfully begins before you take the club in your hand. Because of the size of a driver—it has the largest head of any club—you must tee up the ball properly. You also must position the ball in the most strategic part of the tee box area to improve your chances of hitting the fairway.

## Tees

Because your driver has the largest clubface of any club, and because it should make contact with the ball on a slight upswing, you need to tee the ball up higher than you would with any other club. Using a longer tee (see page 35) helps you do so.

By putting the ball on the tee just above where the clubface sits when you address the ball, you will be able to strike it on a slight upswing, ideally in the center of the clubface.

In some instances, you should tee the ball lower when using a driver, such as when you are hitting into a strong wind (you want the ball to fly lower to reduce the wind's effect). If you have a steep downswing, which makes the club come into the ball at a sharp angle, teeing it lower helps you avoid hitting underneath the ball, which produces a pop-up into the air without much distance.

## The Tee Box

Every hole on the course has a tee box—an area defined by two markers that indicate where you can tee up your first shot. It's illegal to tee the ball up in front of or outside these markers—if you do so during an official competition, you will incur a penalty. However, if your ball is within the defined tee box area, your feet can be outside the markers as you take your tee shot.

To hole ⟶

You are allowed to tee the ball anywhere between the two markers and as far as two club lengths back from each of the markers.

You can also use the tee box to your advantage depending on the shape of the fairway you're trying to hit. Be aware of the natural shape of your shot: If you tend to slice or hook, factor that tendency into where you tee up the ball.

For example, if you're hitting onto a fairway that has water or bunkers on the right side and you naturally slice the ball (curving from left to right), tee up your ball on the right side of the tee box. Doing so will make the fairway "wider" visually, enabling you to start the ball flight away from the hazard and giving you more confidence in landing the ball away from the hazard.

Because the driver is the longest club you will own (other than a long putter), the swing you make with it will be bigger, wider, and longer than any other.

There are three main points to keep in mind in order to make a good swing with a driver:

- Keep your head behind the ball from start to finish.
- Put 60 percent of your weight on your right foot since the ball is forward in your stance and the ball is on a tee.
- Make sure that your left shoulder starts slightly higher than your right (which should happen naturally since your right hand is lower on the club than your left).

### STANCE

Position the ball off the inside of your left heel. Your head should be just behind the ball, but your hands need to be directly in line with the ball. Your grip should tilt your shoulders so that your left shoulder is slightly higher than your right one. Your feet should be shoulder width apart.

Head behind ball

Left shoulder higher than right

Hands in line with ball

Feet shoulder width apart

60% of weight on right foot

## FIRST MOVE

To begin your swing, your hands, arms, shoulders, and the clubhead should turn back and inside away from the ball, with your wrists beginning to hinge.

## HALFWAY BACK

As you move the club farther back, your wrists hinge more as your hands move toward your right hip. The club should be at a 45-degree angle to your right hip, with your weight slowly moving into your right heel.

### TIP

To feel a proper wrist hinge, grip a club and hold it straight out in front of you. Then point the club straight up in the air (your thumbs should be pointing up). You've just "hinged your wrists." An improper hinge makes the wrists point to the left or right.

*CONTINUED ON NEXT PAGE*

## TOP OF BACKSWING

At the top of your backswing, the shaft of the club should be roughly parallel to the ground. That depends on your own range of motion—more flexible golfers could take the shaft past parallel, while less flexible golfers might not be able to reach parallel. Ideally, your left arm at this point should be as long as it was at address. Your left shoulder should be behind the ball to make a full turn, and the clubhead should be pointing in the general direction of the target. Most of your weight should be toward the inside of your right heel.

## STARTING DOWNSWING

As you begin your downswing, you should feel as if the center of your body is unwinding while your head stays back. The grip end of the club should be moving downward along an inside path toward the ball, and your weight should start moving into your left foot.

As you reach this position, your hands will be driving the grip end of the club to the ball. Notice that the clubhead is lagging behind your hands and your knees are still facing the ball.

## IMPACT

At impact, your head should be behind the club. Your left arm, your left shoulder, and the club should form a straight line coming up from the ball. The inside of your right foot should still be on the ground, and your hips and belt buckle should have rotated toward the target.

## HALFWAY THROUGH

Just after impact, the club should be pointing toward the target. Your right heel will be coming up off the ground, and your right wrist will have rolled over your left wrist.

*CONTINUED ON NEXT PAGE*

## FINISH

At the finish, all your weight should be over your left heel. Your right shoulder should be lower than your left, just as when you started the swing. The shaft of the club should be right behind your neck. Your right heel will be up in the air, with only the right toe touching the ground, and your belt buckle should be pointing toward the target. (That will depend on your flexibility: The belt buckle could be more left for those with a greater range of motion, or more right for those who are less flexible. Either way is generally okay.)

A balanced finish is critical to completing a good swing. Without balance, you will not be able to successfully repeat the swing on a consistent basis. While the position may be uncomfortable when you are just beginning to play, you will need to practice it and get your body used to supporting your weight in that position.

To work on your swing balance, close your eyes for an entire practice swing and hold the finish position for five seconds without opening your eyes. Being able to do so is a good indication of your ability to make a balanced swing.

## TIP

To see whether you have struck the ball on the proper part of the clubface, check the underside of your driver. Many times, a painted tee will leave a mark there. (Natural wood-colored tees won't leave marks.) That mark indicates where the club hit the tee, giving you a good idea of how close to the center of the clubhead you managed to strike the ball.

The yardage and width of a hole will help you determine which club to use from the tee box.

On par-fours and par-fives with wide, generous fairways, you will want to use a driver so that you can hit the ball as far as possible. On shorter par-fours and on holes with narrower fairways, consider using a fairway wood, a hybrid club, or even an iron. You will sacrifice distance but will probably gain accuracy and improve your position for the next shot. The higher the club's loft, the less sidespin it puts on the ball, and the better chance the ball has of traveling straight. Of course, you still have to make a good swing!

Here are some other points to keep in mind when selecting a club with which to tee off:

- Your long shot can roll through a fairway and wind up in the rough or even in a hazard. An accurate player will always be a more consistent player.

- You want your drive to end up on a level lie in the fairway. Take into account the distance you usually hit the ball and where the shot may finish.

- Always take into account the position of the hazards (sand, water, heavy rough, and so on) before deciding which club to hit.

- Not many beginners (or more experienced players, for that matter) can reach a par-five green in two shots. Plan your tee shot with your second and third shots in mind, leaving yourself comfortable distances to hit before you reach the green.

## TIP

If you're not sure whether you can reach the green on a par-three with a particular club, choose the next lowest-lofted club (for example, a 6-iron instead of a 7-iron) and tee the ball up a club length or two behind the tee markers. Doing so helps remove the indecision, and you'll make a more confident swing.

Always tee the ball up for your first shot on a hole, whether you are using a driver, a wood, a hybrid club, or an iron. While more experienced players might not use a tee when playing a par-three, beginners should always do so to help get the ball up into the air.

# Tee Shot Routine

Since your tee shot is the first shot you take on any hole, picking a target and executing a good swing are essential to scoring well. Using the same routine every time you hit a tee shot—and any other shot, for that matter—will help you make a consistent, repeatable swing.

## Keep It Consistent

After teeing your ball up in the tee box, stand behind it and look at your target. Take into account where the hazards, if any, are located. Also note your potential landing area and the distance of the next shot you would face from that point.

As you step in to take your stance, first with your right foot and then with your left, take another look at your target to ensure that you are lined up properly.

As you stand over the ball, "waggle" the club—move it back and forth slightly—without touching the ball. Doing so will help ease tension in your hands and arms, helping you make a fuller, more relaxed swing.

Right before you begin your swing, look again at the target to visualize the ball going right at it.

Then make a balanced swing and watch your ball land in the fairway!

# Practice Drills

Driving is the ultimate combination of power and accuracy. Staying in control and in balance during the swing is an important key to finding the fairway. These drills will help you achieve that goal.

## Hear the Swoosh

To ensure that your driver (or any other club's) swing reaches its fastest point at the very bottom of the swing, listen for the swoosh sound. Take any club, and instead of holding it at the grip end, hold it toward the clubhead end. Then make a regular swing without hitting a ball or allowing the club to touch the ground.

No sound

Swoosh

If you hear a swoosh early in the backswing, you are releasing the energy behind the swing too early and losing the proper angle. This usually results in an over-the-top swing that can produce a slice or hook.

Ideally, you should hear the sound just as the club passes where the ball would normally be on the ground.

## The Shadow Knows

Because the driver is the longest club you will use for a tee shot, the chance of getting your head in front of the ball prior to impact is greater. It's very important to keep your head behind the ball, even slightly after impact. To make sure that your head stays in the proper position, try this drill:

1. Stand in a spot where your body casts a shadow out in front of you.

2. Address the ball as if you were going to make a swing. Look at your shadow to make sure that your head is behind the ball.

3. Take some practice swings. While doing so, look at your shadow again to make sure that your head remains behind the ball throughout your swing. (It's okay for your head to move forward at the completion of the swing.)

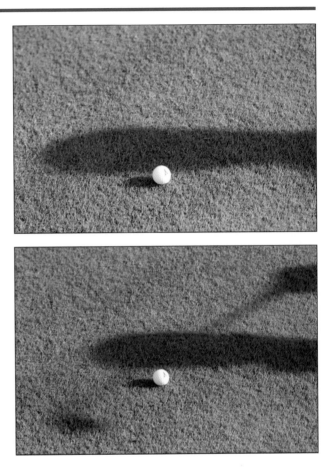

# chapter 6

# Chipping and Pitching

The majority of shots you hit during a round of golf are from 100 yards and closer to the hole. If your short game—largely made up of chipping and pitching—is not good, chances are your score will suffer the consequences. This chapter discusses how to chip and pitch the ball from the fairway and the rough, explains the stance and swing you use to execute these shots, and suggests some practice drills to help you improve your skills.

A chip shot is a low, rolling shot that travels farther on the ground than it does in the air. You use this shot to advance the ball a short distance (35 yards or less) onto the green from the fairway or the fringe around the green. You can also chip from the rough if there is no bunker, water, or other hazard between you and your target.

A chip shot is recommended over a pitch shot (see page 95) in these situations because it has a lower trajectory, giving you a better idea of how the ball will react when it lands. A higher trajectory means that the ball is spinning more, and it's harder to predict how the ball will land and then roll. The chipping swing also requires less motion than the pitching swing, which means that fewer things can go wrong. So, whenever possible, go low with a chip shot.

## Choose a Club for Chipping

You can use a variety of clubs to hit a chip shot, depending on the length of the shot and the placement of the pin. A 9-iron is a great club for a beginner to use because it has enough loft to get the ball into the air but still allows it to roll on the green. Less-lofted clubs provide even more control for chip shots, where you are trying to land the ball quickly and let it roll toward the target instead of trying to land the ball directly at or near the target. You should use one of these clubs when there is a good bit of room on the green between yourself and the hole—for example, when you are trying to chip to a hole on the opposite side of the green. A hybrid club is another good chipping option because its wider sole enables it to glide across the grass.

A sand wedge has more loft than these clubs and will get the ball into the air quickly, making it more suitable for pitching than for chipping.

### TIP

When facing a short fairway shot from just off the green that's not obstructed by hazards or rough, your first choice should be to putt. If conditions allow, putting will keep the ball on the ground for the entire shot, reducing the potential of a bad bounce that may impair a chip shot or pitch shot.

Unless you're standing on an uphill or downhill slope, or the ball is above or below your feet, your stance should be the same for all chip shots.

Here are six key elements of the chipping stance:

- Position the ball toward your back foot.

- Make sure that the grip end of the club is farther forward than the clubhead (which will make the shaft of the club lean forward toward the target, ahead of the ball). Your hands should be in line with the crease of your left pant leg.

- Grip down 2 inches from the end of the club.

- Shift your weight toward your front foot.

- Keep your nose in front of the ball, not behind it.

- Use an open stance to help your hips and legs clear through the swing and enable the club to come back around to your left side. (In an open stance, a line drawn across the toes of both feet would point to the left of your target.) Although the chipping swing is much shorter than a full swing, you still need to follow through to the finish. The clubhead may not travel more than a few feet past where the ball was, but your hips still need to rotate toward the target at the end of the swing, as shown on the opposite page. If your belt buckle is still facing where the ball was on the ground, you will likely hit the ground before hitting the ball.

After you take your stance, visualize the spot where you want the ball to land, look at the ball, begin your backswing, swing through the ball, and complete your follow-through.

Nose in front of ball

Grip end ahead of clubhead

Ball toward back foot

Weight toward front foot

**TIP**

If you find that you're hitting the top of the ball when chipping, move the ball a bit farther back in your stance. Doing so will help you make a descending blow right behind the ball.

The swing for chipping is similar to a putting stroke (see Chapter 8). It's simple—much less complicated than a full swing.

During a chipping swing, you want to keep the club low as you swing back and follow through. In fact, you never need to swing above your knees when chipping.

To visualize those limits, think of a clock face: If your ball is at 6:00, then your backswing would not go past 4:00 (assuming that the clock is facing you), and your follow-through would not go past 8:00.

During a chip shot, your left arm and the club's shaft should act as one lever-type mechanism. Always try to brush the turf after striking the ball with a descending blow. The swing itself is a miniature version of a full swing: The club travels away from the ball on a slight arc to the inside, comes back to square at impact, and then travels back to the inside after impact. (See pages 72–73 for more on the swing path.)

**TIP**

Always take a practice swing and make contact with the ground before chipping. Doing so will encourage the feeling associated with a descending blow.

If your approach shot lands short of the green but remains in the fairway, you can chip the ball from that spot. This shot is called a *bump and run*, where the ball lands on the ground again soon after leaving the clubface and rolls toward the target.

With a fairway chip, you have a choice of clubs to hit with. The longer the distance you want to cover, the lower the iron you can use. An 8-iron can be used for a 30-yard or longer chip. A lower-numbered iron has less loft, which will help keep your ball lower to the ground than a higher-numbered iron with more loft.

You should go farther on your backswing and follow-through as the distance you are chipping increases, but never to the point of making a full swing.

Pitching wedge
9-iron
8-iron

As with any other chip shot, you need to determine where you want the ball to land and begin rolling toward the target. If the hole is close to the front edge of the green, you want to land the ball on the fairway and let it roll to the cup. If the hole is on the far side of the green, try to land the ball on the green itself and let the ball roll to the cup from there. You also need to keep in mind how the natural break of the green, if any, will affect your chip. Just as you would read the green for putting purposes (see Chapter 8), read the green when chipping. Factor in the topography of the green—whether it slopes uphill, downhill, to the left, or to the right—when determining the appropriate landing area for the ball.

# Chipping from the Rough

The type of lie you have determines the type of chip shot you make from the rough. A chip from light rough will "release"—or roll upon landing on the green—differently than one that is hit from deep rough. You use the same swing as for a greenside chip.

## Tips for Chipping from the Rough

- If the ball is sitting up and the grass is growing in the direction of the hole, use a pitching wedge, 9-iron, or 8-iron.
- If the ball is nestled deep within the grass and the grass is growing away from the hole, use a sand wedge.
- If the ball is in heavy rough, play it more in the middle of your stance to help you get some loft, and make a more aggressive swing.

Chips hit from the rough tend to finish farther than similar shots hit from the fairway. When grass comes between the ball and the clubface, the ball does not spin as much as it would after being hit from the fairway. That makes choosing the right club and picking the best landing area very important.

A pitch shot is a shot hit from around or close to the green that travels on a higher trajectory than a chip shot. This shot helps your ball fly over bunkers, water hazards, or rough and get close to the hole. Because you use a high-lofted club for this shot, the ball receives extra spin, giving it both height and the capability to stop quickly once it lands, instead of rolling along the green as a chip shot would.

When you have to pitch over a bunker or water hazard to the green, you need to use a higher-lofted club, like a pitching wedge or sand wedge (or, when your skills improve, a lob wedge, since that club has the highest degree of loft). The higher loft ensures that the ball has enough trajectory to clear the hazard and land safely on the green.

# Pitching Stance

Pitch shots require a wider stance than chip shots because you transfer more of your weight from back to front during the swing. You also want to grip down 1 inch on the club and shift your weight toward your left side.

## Set Up

The position of the ball in relation to your feet will change depending on the type of trajectory you want the ball to have. There are three main positions to consider, depending on whether you want to hit a low-trajectory, medium-trajectory, or high-trajectory pitch shot.

First, stand with the ball in middle of your feet, with your heels together. Your feet should point out in opposite directions and form a V-shape. From this position, you can adjust one or both of your feet to hit a low-, medium-, or high-trajectory pitch shot. Note that your stance should be slightly open, with your hips and shoulders pointing just left of the target in line with your feet.

## Low-Trajectory Pitch Shot

To hit a low-trajectory pitch shot, move your left foot forward toward the target. The ball should then be toward the back of your stance. The club shaft should lean forward ahead of the ball, and your hands should be positioned toward your left thigh. The follow-through on this shot remains below your waist.

*CONTINUED ON NEXT PAGE*

**TIP**

To get more roll, play the ball toward your right foot. To get more loft, play the ball toward your left foot. Think "right for roll, left for loft."

### Medium-Trajectory Pitch Shot

To hit a medium-trajectory pitch shot, take equal steps side to side so that the ball is in the middle of your stance. The club shaft should be in line with the ball or just slightly ahead of it, and your hands should be right in front of your zipper. Your follow-through should end waist-high.

# chapter 6

## High-Trajectory Pitch Shot

To hit a high-trajectory pitch shot, move your right foot back away from the target so that the ball is forward in your stance. The club shaft should be just behind the ball, and your hands just to the right of your belly button. Maintain a smooth tempo throughout the swing, and unhinge your wrists at impact to help add loft to the shot.

**TIP**

Depending on the lie you have and the club you use, the amount of roll for a pitch shot will differ by trajectory. With a sand wedge, approximate roll distances are 15 feet (high trajectory), 20 to 30 feet (medium trajectory), and more than 30 feet (low trajectory).

# Pitching Swing

**The players who hit the best pitch shots have a rhythmic swing, maintaining a smooth tempo on both the backswing and the downswing. A common mistake is to take a very fast downswing, which usually results in a poor shot. Think of maintaining a steady motion, with your follow-through at least as long as your backswing.**

A common pitch shot involves hitting over a greenside bunker. To hit this shot successfully, take a wide stance and relax your arms, letting them "stay long." Hinge your wrists rather than bend your left elbow, using the loft of the club to get the ball up into the air.

Take a very big backswing with a full shoulder turn, using approximately 50 percent of your energy. Hinge your wrists early in your backswing.

Throughout the swing, keep your weight toward your left foot.

 **TIP**

Try to count the same numbers (such as 1-2-3) during your backswing and again as you swing to the finish. Doing so will help you build a smooth tempo and avoid a jerky swing.

At impact, the muscles in your wrists should feel relaxed while your hands hold the club firmly, but not tightly. Your arms should feel loose and long when you strike the ball.

As you finish the swing, the club should end up high over your left shoulder.

# Practice Drills

Both chip shots and pitch shots require a tremendous amount of touch to get the ball close to the target. Practicing these types of shots is very important in reducing the number of strokes you take near the green—a sure way to improve your overall score. Here are some practice drills that will help you build your chipping and pitching skills.

## Chipping Drill

To help you practice an important part of chipping—not breaking your wrists at impact—take two clubs together in your hands, holding one in the regular position on the grip and the other on the shaft close to the clubhead, as shown.

Doing so keeps your wrists out of the shot and enables your left arm and the club to act as one; your left arm is essentially an extension of the club. This drill prevents you from breaking your wrists at impact. If you do, you will feel the shaft of the club hit your ribcage at impact. If done properly, that club will never make contact with your body. You might be trying too hard to get the ball into the air; instead, you should let the club's loft do the work.

## Pitching Drill

For this drill, place two tees next to each other 2 inches behind the ball. Practice hitting down on the ball by avoiding contact with the two tees. You are trying to make a descending blow at impact. If you don't, you will likely top the ball and hit a line drive that sails far past your target.

If you swing incorrectly, your club will hit one or both of the tees prior to hitting the ball.

### TIP

For pitching or chipping, your left arm and the club should form a straight line, from the club shaft all the way down to the ball, at and shortly after impact, as shown in the left-hand photo on the opposite page. Do not hinge your wrists, as shown here.

# Bunker Shots

Playing in the sand at the beach is fun. Playing in the sand on a golf course? Not so much. Unfortunately, sand—collected in bunkers—is a hazard you will encounter on every course. Built in all shapes and sizes, bunkers are placed along the edges (and sometimes in the middle) of fairways, as well as around greens, collecting mis-hit and misdirected shots like magnets. Unlike hitting a ball into a water hazard, though, you have a chance to save a stroke by getting out of a bunker successfully. This chapter discusses the different types of bunkers you will encounter and how you can hit shots out of them.

# Types of Bunkers

There are three types of bunkers waiting to capture your ball: fairway bunkers, greenside bunkers, and waste areas. While some golfers are convinced that bunkers are lined with ball magnets—why else would their shots always end up there?—there's no need to dig into the sand and check. The purpose of bunkers is threefold: strategy, beauty, and a bit of mental anguish for those who find their way into one. You're supposed to avoid them, after all!

## FAIRWAY BUNKERS

Fairway bunkers, which are longer and shallower than greenside bunkers, are usually found on one or both sides of a fairway. Course designers frequently place a bunker at the corner of a dogleg hole (a hole that bends to the right or left) to increase the risk for players attempting to take the shortest path to the hole. Bunkers are sometimes placed in the middle of a fairway as well.

## GREENSIDE BUNKERS

Greenside bunkers can be located at the front, side, or back of a green. As the last line of defense for a hole, these bunkers are usually deeper and steeper than others found on the course, requiring a more skillful shot to get the ball up over the lip and onto the putting surface.

## WASTE AREAS

You may also come across waste areas. Mostly found on courses in desert-style settings, these sandy areas differ from fairway and greenside bunkers in that they are usually not maintained (so they do not need to be raked) and can be walked through—and sometimes driven through by carts. Unlike fairway and greenside bunkers, you may ground your club in a waste area before taking your shot (see page 113).

**TIP**

Always enter a bunker at its lowest point. Never jump into a bunker. Doing so can damage the bunker, not to mention your own body.

After hitting your shot, make sure to rake the bunker, including your footprints, leaving it as neat as you found it.

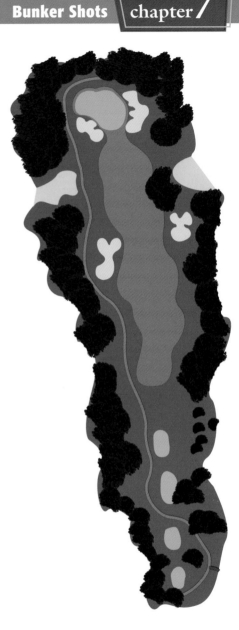

# Hit Out of a Greenside Bunker

To get your ball out of a greenside bunker, you need to use the right club, maintain a good stance, enter the sand with your club at the right spot, and finish the swing properly. And the club should never touch the ball throughout the swing—seriously!

## Use the Right Club

Your club choice for a greenside bunker shot is easy: either a sand wedge or a lob wedge. But these clubs need to have the proper amount of loft and "bounce," or else the likelihood of your getting the ball up and out of the bunker decreases.

A wedge is built with bounce in the sole, or underside of the club, which enables it to go through the sand smoothly. The leading edge of the wedge cuts through the sand, and the angle of the sole (the bounce) acts as a rudder. The bounce helps push the club back up out of the sand. Not enough bounce can cause the club to dig into the sand instead of gliding through it, resulting in "fat" or "chunked" shots that do not leave the bunker.

### TIP

As a beginner, look for a sand wedge with at least 54 degrees of loft and more than 10 degrees of bounce. As your bunker skills improve, you may want to add another wedge, purchased separately, with a higher degree of loft and less bounce. Look for a wedge that has 60 degrees of loft and 6 degrees of bounce.

# chapter 7

## Adjust Your Stance

For stability purposes, your greenside bunker stance should be slightly wider than for a normal fairway shot. Position the ball just ahead of center between your feet. Dig your feet into the sand (more so than in a fairway bunker) to help maintain your balance. Doing so is especially important if your ball is on an uphill or downhill lie.

For a greenside bunker stance, most of your weight should be on your front foot. Open the clubface slightly to let the bounce of the club do its job of driving up and out of the sand after entry.

Your stance should be open slightly to the target line. If your stance is too open, however, the club will skim the sand and glance across the ball itself, resulting in a line-drive shot that sails past the hole or even over the green.

*CONTINUED ON NEXT PAGE*

## Swing the Club

The greenside bunker swing is very similar to your standard swing from the fairway (see Chapter 4), with your wrists hinged early in the backswing.

Since you will be facing a short shot from a greenside bunker, your backswing doesn't need to go too far back. For longer greenside bunker shots, however, the length of your swing should increase accordingly, and your stance and clubface should be less open.

Keep in mind that you should hear a thump as your club slides through the sand, resulting in a shot that comes out high and lands softly. If your swing is too steep, then the club will dig too deep into the sand and not propel the ball upward—leaving you with another sand shot.

Accelerate through the shot; do not slow down as your club enters the sand. You are trying to splash sand out of the bunker; if you don't do that, the ball won't move.

At the very bottom of your swing (the point where your downswing ends and your follow-through begins), the club should hit the sand first. Because the quality of sand used in bunkers differs from course to course, the point at which your club should enter the sand will vary slightly. If the sand is very fluffy, you want to enter it a bit farther behind the ball than you would if the sand were wet and compact.

Your posture during a greenside bunker shot is different than for a fairway bunker shot. Here, your feet are a bit farther apart, and your knees are flexed a bit more.

*CONTINUED ON NEXT PAGE*

Your hands should be even with or slightly behind the clubhead at impact.

If your hands are ahead of the club, the clubhead will dig into the sand, reducing the effectiveness of the club's bounce.

Your club should not touch the ball at any time during a greenside bunker shot. There is no penalty if it does, but you should be aiming for a spot approximately 1 inch behind the ball. Although you need to swing the clubhead through the sand on this shot, remember that your club cannot touch the sand or the ball *prior to* your swing. This is known as grounding your club. If you do so, you will incur a penalty stroke.

The wedge will cut through the sand underneath the ball, lifting it up into the air without actually making contact with it.

***CONTINUED ON NEXT PAGE***

## Follow Through

A good follow-through is essential to a successful bunker shot. Stopping at impact will affect the distance and height of the shot. Completing the swing with your hands and club high in the air should result in a more powerful swing and generate the force you need to advance the ball out of the bunker.

A proper finish means staying in balance with your weight over your front foot.

You should not be leaning backward at the finish unless you are hitting from an uphill lie.

There are a few major differences between a greenside bunker shot and a fairway bunker shot that you need to keep in mind.

## Fairway Bunker Shots vs. Greenside Bunker Shots

- During a fairway bunker shot, you hit the ball first, not the sand first. You are trying to pick the ball cleanly off the sand and leave a divot mark *in front of* where your ball was positioned, not behind or directly under it.

- In a fairway bunker, you should stand tall with your feet dug into the sand only slightly for balance. Your legs should do less work than in a greenside bunker. The idea is to keep your lower body "quiet," or as still as possible. Consequently, you must take at least one more club than you would normally use to cover your desired distance. For example, if you would ordinarily hit a 7-iron from that distance, you'll want to use a 6-iron to hit out of the bunker.

- You take a longer, fuller swing in a fairway bunker than in a greenside bunker.

- For a greenside bunker shot, your goal is to land the ball on the green. For a fairway bunker shot, you may not be able to reach the green. Study the hole and plan your fairway bunker shot based on where you want to play your next shot from.

# Bunker Lies

The type of lie you have in a bunker determines how your ball will react after you complete the swing.

## How Does Your Ball Lie?

### STANDARD

Sitting on top of the sand—almost as if the ball is teed up—is the best possible position for the ball to be in. It provides an excellent chance for you to slide your wedge through the sand underneath the ball. From this lie, the ball will *check,* or quickly stop rolling on the green, due to spin. Make sure that your target landing area is fairly close to the cup.

### BURIED

A high shot that lands directly in a bunker, especially one filled with very soft sand, can end up "buried," or as a "fried egg" (since that's what it looks like). This type of lie requires a more closed clubface to offset the amount of sand around the ball. You can expect the ball to come out low with lots of roll from this lie, so make sure to pick a landing area well short of your target.

## UPHILL

If your ball sits on an uphill slope in a bunker, you need to adjust your stance accordingly. The tendency is to lean into the sand and keep your shoulders perpendicular to the horizon, but doing so will cause the club to dig into the sand and the ball to go nowhere.

*Wrong*

Instead, your shoulders should tilt in the direction of the lie both in your stance and throughout your swing. Your weight is mostly on your back foot, but not so much that you lose your balance. Because of the higher trajectory it should have, the ball will land softly on the green without much roll, so make sure to pick a landing area very close to your target.

**CONTINUED ON NEXT PAGE**

*Correct*

## DOWNHILL

If your ball rests on a downhill slope in a bunker, you need to adjust your stance accordingly. The tendency is to lean into the sand and keep your shoulders perpendicular to the horizon.

*Wrong*

Instead, your shoulders should tilt downward in the direction of the lie both in your stance and throughout your swing. Your weight is mostly on your front foot, but not so much that you lose your balance. This shot will have a lower trajectory and therefore more roll when it lands on the green, so make sure to pick a landing area well short of your target. To offset the lower trajectory, open the clubface and aim your feet slightly left of the target.

*Correct*

Here are two practice drills for greenside bunker shots. You don't even need a ball!

### HIT THE LINE

Draw two lines in the sand an inch or two apart. Try to hit the first line with your club, and make sure that your divot carries through the second line (where your ball would normally be positioned). Look at the mark you make after each swing. If you hit between the lines or hit the second line first, you will not execute a proper greenside bunker shot. Hitting the first line ensures that your club has entered the sand at the proper point so that it will go underneath the ball.

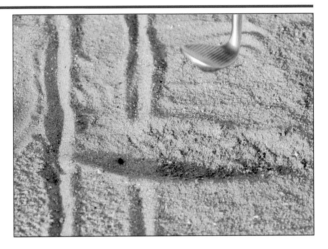

### SPLASH AROUND

During a successful greenside bunker shot, the sand will splash forward after being hit by your club. Without using a ball, swing your wedge in a bunker and practice that sensation of splashing the sand out of the bunker. Be sure to rake the bunker after you're done!

# Putting

Getting the ball into the hole in as few strokes as possible is the ultimate goal of golf. The final step in that process comes on the green, where the art of putting determines your score for each hole. In fact, putts make up almost half of your score during every round. Every putting surface is different, but having a basic understanding of how to read greens and putt will improve your score dramatically. This chapter discusses how you grip the putter, the proper putting stance and swing, and specific goals for different types of putts. We also give you some practice drills to help you hone your putting skills.

# How to Putt

Putting requires the same essential skills as any other swing you make: balance, tempo, good mechanics, and concentration. If you don't hit the ball a long way, putting can be a great equalizer when it comes to scoring. Assuming that your putter fits you properly and your setup is good, you should be able to make a good stroke and roll the ball into the hole in as few putts as possible.

## Your Putting Routine

That 2-foot putt seems so close to the hole that you may rush your stroke and miss. Then there's the 40-foot putt that seems impossible to make, so you just hit it in the general direction of the hole and hope that you can get your next putt closer. Having a putting routine can help you in both of these situations. Going through the same step-by-step process every time you putt will help you focus on the shot no matter what the distance. Here is the putting routine we recommend:

**1** Mark your ball and study the putt you are facing.

**2** Get low to the ground to read the green and see how the ground is shaped.

   *Note: If other players putt before you, watch their putts to see how they move.*

**3** Choose an intermediate target spot for your putt. If the green is flat, your intermediate target spot will be along the line to the hole itself. If the green slopes to the left or right, your target will be a point along that break where the ball will start to turn toward the hole.

**4** Stand behind or beside the ball and take a practice swing.

**5** Place the putter behind the ball and then take your stance.

**6** Look at your target spot again.

**7** Make your stroke and follow through.

### TIP

After getting into position over the ball, just prior to making your stroke, exhale. Doing so relaxes your muscles and relieves tension— one of the primary reasons for missing putts.

*Mark your ball.*

*Read the green.*

*Take a practice swing.*

*Take your stance.*

**CONTINUED ON NEXT PAGE**

*Address the ball before taking one last look at the target.*

*Take your backswing.*

*Strike the ball.*

*Follow through.*

There are numerous ways to hold the putter—grips include the standard, the cross-handed, and the Claw—but none will be effective for you unless you're comfortable using it. Experiment with each of the grips described below on the practice green to see which one works best.

## Standard Grip

**1** Hang your arms naturally in front of your body so that your palms are open flat and facing each other. Bend forward slightly at the waist so that your eyes are directly over the ball.

**2** Place the putter between your facing palms.

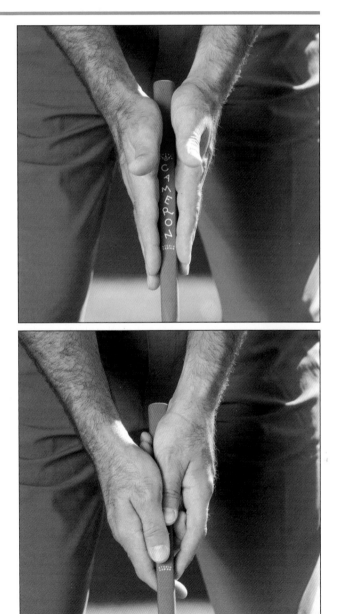

**3** Grasp the putter with both hands. Your thumbs should rest on the front of the putter grip. As with iron shots (see Chapter 4), you can use multiple versions of a grip–for example, cross-handed, the Claw, or the reverse overlap shown here.

However you choose to grip the putter, both hands should work together as one unit. If your hands are apart from each other, then returning the putter to a square position at impact with the ball is much more difficult.

**4** Exert equal (but light) pressure with both hands on the grip throughout the putting stroke.

*CONTINUED ON NEXT PAGE*

## Other Grips

### CROSS-HANDED

Another way to hold the putter is to use a cross-handed grip. It is the same as the standard grip except that you reverse the positions of your hands: Your left hand is on the lower portion of the grip below your right hand (the opposite for lefties). This grip forces you to keep your shoulders more level with the green and helps prevent your wrists from hinging.

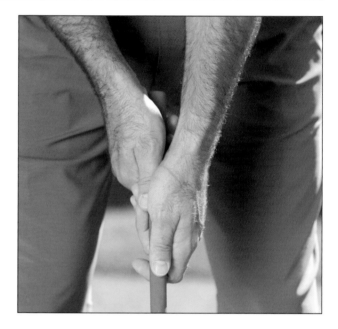

### CLAW

In recent years, players on the PGA Tour have popularized an unorthodox grip dubbed "the Claw." It is a last-resort putting position for players who are not comfortable or successful with other grips. The Claw is designed to help combat the uncertainty of the hand motion during the putting stroke and is one step away from swinging the putter with one hand. The position of the right hand removes any hinging motion in the right wrist. This grip is difficult for beginners to use given its unique hand position.

The top (or left) hand holds the club as in the standard grip, but the club is tucked between the thumb and palm of the lower (right) hand. The right hand does not wrap around the club as in other grips—it remains open and pointing toward the ground in front of the club.

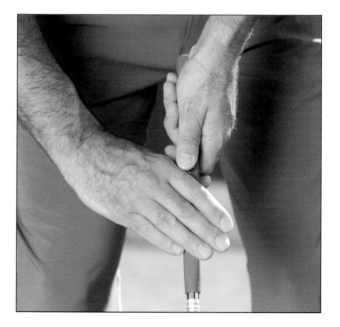

As with your grip, your putting stance should be whatever is most comfortable for you. However, there are elements of a good, basic putting stance that you should adopt.

## Addressing the Ball

**1** Before taking your stance, stand next to or behind the ball, look at the target, and take a practice swing that mirrors the length and tempo required for the putt. Looking at the hole instead of the ball can help you get a feel for the stroke and visualize the path you want the ball to follow.

**2** Take your stance by placing the putter directly behind the ball, aiming at your target. Your arms should hang relaxed and be close to your body, with a little bend in the elbows. Notice how the shaft of the putter and the right forearm are in line; this is the result of a good setup.

*CONTINUED ON NEXT PAGE*

The putter should lie level on the ground when you place it behind the ball. Having the putter flat on the ground gives you the best chance to aim properly.

The toe end of the putter (the end farthest away from you) should not be up in the air when it rests on the ground. This lie angle is too upright; it will cause you to aim left.

Nor should the heel end of the putter (the end closest to you) be up in the air. This lie angle is too flat; it will cause you to aim right.

***Note:*** *If your eyes are over the ball and the heel or toe end of the putter is still up in the air, your putter may not fit you correctly. In that case, talk to a PGA or LPGA professional regarding the length and lie angle of your putter and find out whether you should switch to a different putter.*

③ Once your putter is in position behind the ball, step in first with your right foot and then with your left foot.

Your feet should be no wider than shoulder-width apart—slightly less than that is ideal. Because your ball and your putter are facing directly at the intended path of your putt, your feet and shoulders should be square to that line. Your eyes are directly over the ball.

④ After taking your stance, make sure that the ball is positioned just forward of center between your feet. This setup enables you to strike the ball with a slightly ascending blow, which helps it roll forward consistently. It also reduces any hops or bounces that the ball might take if the putter were to strike it with a descending blow.

**CONTINUED ON NEXT PAGE**

**5** Make sure that the ball is positioned in the middle of the clubface.

Do not line up the ball on the toe or heel end of the putter. Because the mass of the putter is usually located in the center of the clubface, hitting the ball off to either side will decrease the amount of power at impact.

### TIP

To help you line up the ball properly, point the ball's brand name in the direction you are hitting. You can also draw a line around the ball to help you with alignment. Doing so also enables you to learn whether you struck the ball in the middle of the club-face. If the ball rolls with the line spinning end over end straight toward the target, then you hit it solidly in the right spot. If the line wobbles to one side or the other, then you struck the ball off-center.

In a good putting stance, your weight is balanced between both feet or slightly favors the left side. Your arms hang naturally in front of you and your hands are in line with the ball.

You do not want to stand with your hands too far behind the ball, or your wrists will be bent at impact. Doing so adds loft to the putter and causes the ball to bounce or hop after being struck.

# Make the Swing

The putting stroke is shorter and simpler than the other swings you use on the course, but there are still some important things you must do in order to make the putt.

After you get into your stance, but before you take your swing, look one more time at your target line and exhale. Picture your hands and shoulders moving together as one unit. Do not swing with your wrists only.

The amount of backswing you should take depends on the distance of your putt; the longer the putt, the longer the backswing you should use. During the backswing, your head should be steady and your weight should remain as it was at address.

At impact, your hands, your shoulders, and the putter form an upside-down triangle. Keep this position intact throughout the stroke.

Bending your wrists at impact will affect the speed and direction of your putt. If you find yourself doing so, you have taken too long of a backswing, and you will have difficulty controlling speed and accuracy. Your wrists and shoulders should move together, remaining in the upside-down triangle position.

You need to follow through after impact, with the putter passing by your left leg or further depending on the distance of the putt.

Ideally, the length of your backswing will equal the length of your follow-through. For example, if your putter goes back to the pinky toe of your right foot, then it should go forward to the pinky toe of your left foot on the follow-through.

**TIP**

During the backswing, allow the putter to swing slightly to the inside before coming back to square at impact and finishing slightly inside on the follow-through.

# Read the Green

Most greens are made up of multiple sections with slopes that can cause a ball to move right, left, downhill, and/or uphill. That makes *reading the green*—or predicting which way the ball will move after being hit—especially important.

A straight line may be the shortest path to the hole, but the topography of the green often forces the ball to curve away from that path and the hole. This curve is called *break*.

Reading a green starts from the fairway. Study your surroundings as you walk toward the green, because greens often slope in certain directions, such as away from a nearby mountain (a high spot) or toward a body of water (a low spot). Look at the ground the green sits on; you can even study the angle of the cup to get an idea of how the green's surface may slope.

A putt usually breaks left or right to some degree. The break could be dramatic, forcing a wide, curving putt, or subtle, where the ball curves just slightly. Some putts involve a double break, where the ball moves in *both* directions.

The best way to read a green is to look at the putting surface from behind your ball. Make sure your eyes are parallel to the horizon. Crouching down close to the ground will help you see whether the surface is level or tilted in a certain direction. If time and pace of play allow, you can also look at the green from the other direction, with the hole between you and the ball. Walking alongside the area between your ball and the hole is another good way to judge the green's slope. You should also "go to school" on putts hit by other players—see how their balls react to the putting surface and learn what impact those reactions might have on your putt.

Another technique used to read greens is called *plumb bobbing*. This technique involves holding a club up in the air in front of your face and using your dominant eye to determine the amount of break in a putt. For more information about that technique, consult with a PGA or LPGA teaching professional.

The ultimate goal of every putt is to get the ball into the hole. The length of the putt and whether it will travel uphill or downhill affect the power behind your stroke. Judging the direction and speed you have to hit a putt consists of touch, practice, and experience. It's also a matter of "lag putting"—getting the putt at least close to the hole so that you're left with a much shorter and more makeable second (and hopefully final) putt.

## LONG PUTTS

For long putts, distance is more important than accuracy. Imagine a 3-foot circle around the hole—you are aiming at the hole but trying to put enough pace on the ball so that if it doesn't go in, it will come to rest inside that circle, leaving you with a short putt to the hole.

Getting the ball into that 3-foot circle guarantees you a makeable second putt.

An alternate image for long putts is a 3-foot circle directly *behind* the hole. This image can help ensure that your putt reaches the hole or finishes past it, giving you a better chance of making it. A putt that doesn't reach the hole has zero chance of going in. Now there's a classic line heard on golf courses all over the world!

***CONTINUED ON NEXT PAGE***

## UPHILL PUTTS

On uphill putts, pick a point past the hole as your target. (In the photo, the tee marking the target is beyond the hole and allows for a right-to-left break.) Doing so will ensure that you hit the ball firmly enough that it will go up the hill and ideally stop in or near the hole, as opposed to stopping short of the hole or even rolling back down the hill.

## DOWNHILL PUTTS

On downhill putts, pick a spot in front of the hole as your target, as indicated by the tee in the photo. Doing so enables the natural slope of the green to carry the ball the rest of the way without it going too far past the hole if it doesn't go in.

## PUTTING FROM THE FRINGE

Putting from the *fringe*—the closely mown turf immediately surrounding the putting surface—is an added challenge when it comes to distance control. Because fringe grass is slightly higher than the actual putting surface, you need to strike the ball firmly in order to move it onto the green. The fringe grass will take speed off the putt immediately, so you must increase the length of your backswing accordingly.

## PUTTING FROM THE FAIRWAY

Some holes have an open entrance to the green, without high grass, water hazards, or bunkers that normally would prevent you from putting directly from the fairway toward the hole. Check the condition of the grass in this area to judge the pace needed to get the ball onto the green and close to the hole. The higher the grass, the more speed is needed. If there is a sprinkler head in your line, or if the condition of the grass is inconsistent, then it's better to chip the ball (see Chapter 6).

**TIP**

If your ball is up against the *collar* (where the fairway or greenside rough meets the fringe of the green), or the fringe grass is especially long, see page 184 to play the shot with a putter, or consider these options. You could use a wedge and hit the ball with the bottom edge (called *blading*) to avoid getting caught in the grass. Or you could use a hybrid, 5-wood, or 7-wood—the larger clubhead will move through the grass more easily than a putter. If you use one of those clubs, choke down on the grip, keep the ball in the center of your stance, and stand closer to the ball than you normally would when using those clubs.

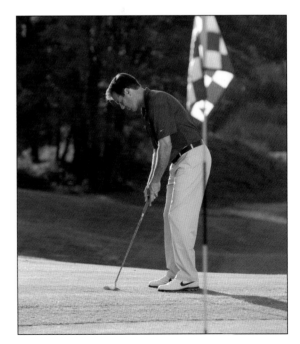

The best part about practicing your putting is that you don't need a driving range. You can use virtually any surface (your living room carpet, a hallway, etc.) and substitute a cup for the hole to roll some putts and practice your routine. The ideal venue is a practice green, but you can try these drills anywhere. The important thing is to practice!

## TENNIS BALL PUTTING

Try practice putting with a tennis ball from short distances. After doing so, the hole will look significantly larger to your eye when you go back to using a golf ball.

## EYE POSITION

Lay a CD (don't use one from your favorite band, though!) upside-down on the ground and place a golf ball directly in the middle of it. When you take your stance over the ball, you should be able to see your eyes reflected in the CD. If you can't, then your head is not in the correct position. Turn back to page 127 and review the information on the putting stance.

## DISTANCE CONTROL

To work on your distance control, place three tees in the ground—one 5 feet away, the next 2 feet to the right and 15 feet away, and the third another 2 feet to the right and 30 feet away from you. Alternate hitting putts to each tee to help develop your feel for distance.

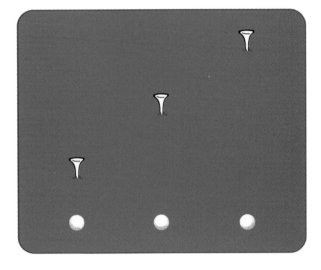

## AROUND THE WORLD

Encircle a hole with balls at a short distance (say 3 feet) and move around the circle putting the balls into the hole. This repetitive drill will help you develop both feel and confidence on short putts. If you set up this drill on a hole that has a lot of slope, you will get a crash course in reading greens.

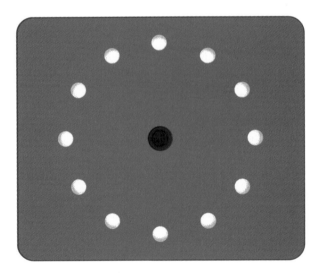

# At the Course

Every golf course consists of the same basic elements: tees, fairways, bunkers, and greens. But each course follows certain rules and regulations, all of which you need to know before stepping up to the first tee and playing away. Once you do tee off, understanding the basic rules and etiquette of the game and the correct way to keep score will help ensure that you do your part to maintain the proper pace of play and enjoy the sport as it was meant to be played.

This chapter describes the steps you need to follow after you arrive at the course, the rules you absolutely need to know, and the right way to keep track of the strokes you take.

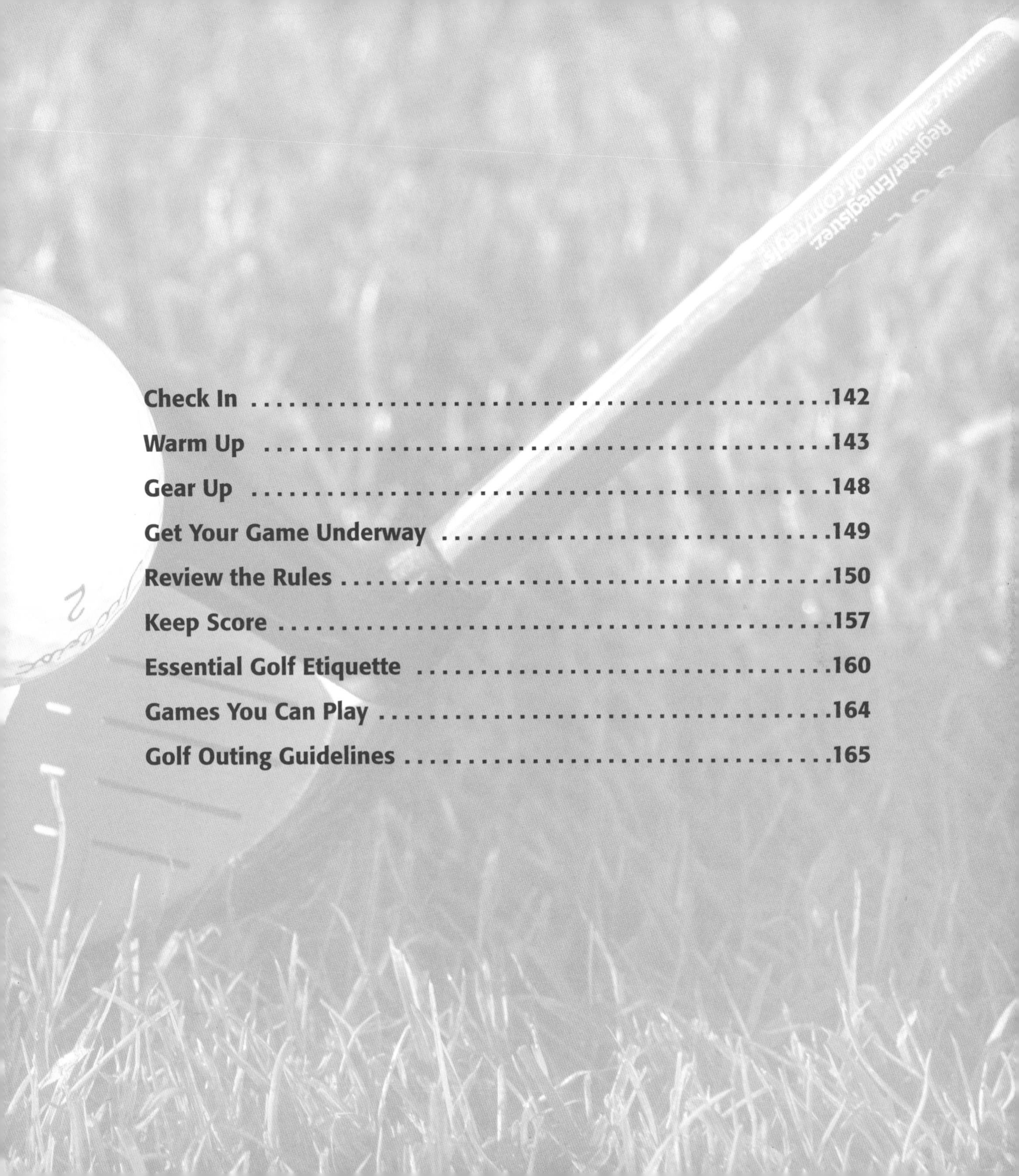

You've found a course that you want to play, your clubs are in the car, and you have called ahead to arrange for a tee time. Now what? From where to put your clubs to whom you need to see before playing, this section covers the check-in process from start to finish.

## BAG DROP

Upon arriving at the course, you will usually find an area just outside the clubhouse where you can place your golf bag prior to entering the building. Often marked with a sign saying "Bag Drop," this is the designated location for golf clubs to be left; do not bring your equipment into the clubhouse. At many courses, you will find someone there to help you; if there is no attendant, inquire inside the clubhouse as to the best location for your clubs.

## CLUBHOUSE AND PRO SHOP

You can't play the course until you check in at the pro shop, located inside the clubhouse. Numerous other facilities are often located within the clubhouse as well, including bathrooms, dining areas, and locker rooms.

The pro shop is where you often pay the required green fees that enable you to play the course. You can also find equipment for sale there—from tees and golf balls to golf clubs and clothing. Yardage books, scorecards, and pencils to use during your round are also often available in the pro shop, although you should find a scorecard and pencil on your golf cart.

## LOCKER ROOM

If the course you are playing has locker rooms, you may change into your golf shoes and appropriate golf attire there. Check with the pro shop staff to see whether you can leave your non-golf shoes or a change of clothes inside a locker or whether you must leave them in your car during your round.

Many facilities frown on golfers changing shoes or clothes in the parking lot and require the use of locker rooms. Call the course ahead of time to find out its policy.

# Warm Up

Always leave yourself time to warm up prior to beginning your round. Whether it's hitting a few practice putts or working through a full bucket of balls with all of your clubs on the practice range, warming up gets you ready to play.

Also important is stretching the muscles you will use while playing—primarily the muscles in your back, shoulders, and legs. This section describes how you can warm up at the course.

## Use the Practice Areas

Virtually every golf course has a practice putting green just outside the clubhouse or near the first tee. Here, you can hit some putts while waiting for the starter to call your group. Keep in mind that this area is often used solely for putting; don't hit chip shots onto the green unless it is permitted.

Many courses also offer a driving range where you can practice hitting balls with your other clubs. You may be hitting off mats or off real grass toward targets in the distance. Check the yardage to each target so that you can accurately gauge how far you are hitting the ball.

You can obtain a bucket of practice range balls (the cost of which is sometimes included in your green fee; otherwise, you must pay for it separately) either in the pro shop or via a machine near the driving range itself. Some pro shops will furnish you with the token needed to obtain practice balls at the machine near the range. Don't worry about picking them up after you've hit them; the range will have a machine that picks up all the balls. In fact, don't leave the designated hitting area to grab an extra ball to hit; it's not worth the potential physical danger.

TODAY'S YARDAGES

| | |
|---|---|
| | 1 9 1 |
| | 1 7 1 |
| | 1 4 1 |
| | 1 2 2 |
| | 8 9 |
| | 7 5 |

FROM THIS POINT

*CONTINUED ON NEXT PAGE*

# Warm Up
## *(continued)*

## Stretch

We can't overemphasize the importance of stretching before playing golf. Warming up loosens muscles, which helps prevent injury and improves your ability to make a proper swing. In fact, it's more important to stretch for five minutes before starting than it is to hit balls on the range for the same amount of time.

Back and wrist injuries are the most common among golfers, especially for women because of their smaller wrists. These injuries are often caused by hitting the ground repeatedly with the club during a practice session or trying to swing through high and heavy rough, among other reasons.

As your flexibility increases, your range of motion will increase. Subtle changes to your swing are likely to take place as you improve. Today, there are even golf-specific exercise therapists who can help build an individualized program for you. Short of doing that, you can do these basic stretches prior to play (and even during the round) to warm up and stay loose.

To help your overall balance and stability during the swing, hold onto a cart or other stable object with your right hand and grasp your left foot or ankle with your left hand. Bring that foot up toward your posterior until you feel a stretch in your thigh, hamstring, and hip. Hold for 15 seconds, and then repeat with the opposite hand and leg.

To help with your hip rotation during the swing, this stretch works on the muscles in and around the hips. Sit on a golf cart (or on the edge of a chair or bench) and place your right ankle on top of your left knee. With your right palm, gently push down on your right knee and hold for 15 seconds. Repeat with the opposite leg and hand.

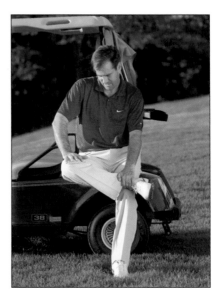

This stretch helps you maintain stability and improves your posture throughout the swing.

1 Standing next to a golf cart, place your right foot on the floor of the cart, with your heel down and your toes in the air.

2 Lean over from the hips and reach toward your toes. Hold that position for 15 seconds to feel a stretch in your calf and hamstring.

3 Repeat with the opposite leg and hand.

Tight shoulders can lead to poor posture and a faulty swing path that forces the club to come over the top of the ball instead of taking a proper inside-square-inside path. This stretch helps the rotation of your shoulders by targeting the rotator cuff area.

1 Hold one end of a club with your left palm facing downward.

2 Grasp the other end of the club with your right palm facing upward.

The club should be pointed upward underneath your right shoulder.

3 Gently pull up with your left hand and hold the stretch for 15 seconds.

4 Repeat with the opposite hands under the other shoulder.

***CONTINUED ON NEXT PAGE***

This torso stretch helps with trunk rotation by stretching the large muscles in your back. A lack of trunk flexibility can lead to improper swing mechanics and potentially even back injury.

 Hold a club straight out in front of you, pointing outward from your chest. Grip the club as far down the shaft as is comfortable.

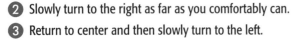 Slowly turn to the right as far as you comfortably can.

Return to center and then slowly turn to the left.

This side stretch helps improve your ability to rotate your body through the swing. Hold any club at opposite ends over your head. Lean to one side and hold for 15 seconds, stretching your oblique and shoulder muscles. Return to vertical and then repeat on the other side.

If you're using a golf cart, grab hold of the back of it and bend forward at the hips, pressing backward with your rear end and holding for 15 seconds. This overall body stretch will help loosen up your shoulders, back, arms, hips, and legs.

There are certain items that you should have in your golf bag at all times. Here's a checklist:

- **Golf clubs:** It doesn't matter so much in a casual round, but the official rules set a limit of 14 clubs per bag. You may own more clubs than that, so consider the course layout when choosing which clubs to leave behind. For example, is it a long course? If so, then carry an extra wood or hybrid club. You can carry fewer clubs as well, especially if you're trying to work on certain shots or increase your comfort level with certain clubs. Plus, if you are walking, bringing fewer than 14 clubs makes your carry bag lighter.

- **Golf balls:** Although golf balls can weigh your bag down in a hurry if you're carrying, make sure that you have several good balls with you, especially if you're playing a course that has deep rough, water hazards, or wooded areas in which balls can easily be lost (or easily found, since your fellow golfers likely have left balls in those very locations).

- **Tees:** It's a good idea to have both long tees (up to 4 inches) for drives and short tees for teeing off on par-three holes. In a pinch, a broken tee can fill in for a short tee. Check the tee box for usable tees left behind by other golfers.

- **Golf glove:** You aren't required to use a glove, but most players choose to wear one to protect their top hand (for righties, the left hand; for lefties, the right) and achieve a better grip. You can also purchase special gloves for various weather conditions: half-fingered gloves for hot days or women with long nails, waterproof gloves for rainy days or women with long nails, etc. Remember to try on gloves before buying to ensure a proper fit.

- **Ball marker:** You can purchase one of these tools individually, but many golf gloves come with a built-in marker that snaps off. You can also use a coin or similar flat object.

- **Divot repair tool:** If your ball lands on the green and makes a dent, this is the tool you use to flatten it out. You wouldn't want your perfect putt to be thrown off-course, so don't leave your own marks behind to spoil other players' putts!

- **Pen or pencil:** Make sure you have something to write with for keeping score and making notes about your round. Short pencils are usually available for free in the pro shop or can be obtained from the starter at the first tee.

- **Protection from the elements:** Bring sunscreen and a hat for sunny days (and cloudy ones—you can still get burned!), and an umbrella if rain is a possibility. Bandages come in handy, too, in case of blisters. Golf clothing is now being made of high-tech materials that wick moisture away from the skin, protect you from the sun's UV rays, and even ward off bugs thanks to insect repellent woven into the fabric.

It's important to clean out your golf bag, ideally after every round but at least once a month, to make sure that you have all the necessary supplies ready for your next round.

You've paid your green fee, you've warmed up, and you're ready to play. But you have one more person to talk to before you can start your round: the starter. You also want to make sure that you have enough food and drinks to maintain your energy throughout the round.

## THE STARTER

After paying your green fee, you may need to check in with the starter. The starter's job is to collect your green fee receipt outside the clubhouse prior to your approaching the first tee. The starter controls access to the first tee; he or she will call your group when appropriate and inform you when to begin play. The starter may also provide you with a scorecard, pencil, yardage book, tees, ball marker, and divot repair tool.

The starter also organizes who you will be playing with. If you are on your own (a "single"), you may be joined by one other person (to form a twosome), two other people (a threesome), or three other people (a foursome). If the course is not busy, you may be allowed to play on your own.

## FOOD AND DRINKS

When it comes to food and drinks at golf courses, you have four options:

- Bring your own.
- Purchase items in the clubhouse prior to playing or after finishing nine holes (the ninth hole usually concludes near the clubhouse).
- Purchase items at the snack shop/halfway house (so called because it is located near the ninth green and the tenth tee when those holes are not located near the clubhouse).
- Look for a beverage cart that makes its way around some courses.

Remember, keeping your energy up is important, as is staying hydrated. If you wait until you feel thirsty, it's usually too late, especially on hot days.

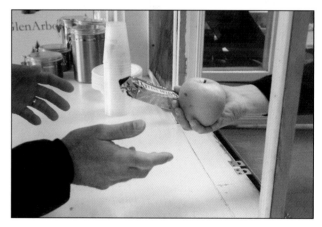

Golf is a game defined by its rules, and every player needs to know the basics before setting out to play. The entire set of rules is best learned by reviewing the United States Golf Association's official rulebook, *The Rules of Golf*, or by going to the USGA's website at www.usga.org.

Short of memorizing the entire rulebook, there are some basic situations that all golfers should understand. This section goes over these situations and discusses what you can and can't do in each one.

## Colored Stakes on the Course

### YELLOW AND RED STAKES

A yellow stake indicates a water hazard. The following options are available if you hit a ball into an area marked with a yellow stake:

- Play the ball as it lies in the hazard. You won't incur a penalty, but do this only if you can take a stance, make contact with the ball, and swing without endangering yourself.

- Play a new ball from behind the hazard anywhere on a line from the hole back to the point where the ball crossed into the hazard (one-stroke penalty).

- Play a new ball from the spot from which you hit the original ball that entered the hazard (one-stroke penalty).

If you hit your ball into a hazard defined by red stakes, you have two additional options to choose from:

- Play a new ball from up to two club lengths away—but no closer to the hole—from the point where the ball entered the hazard (one-stroke penalty).

- Drop a ball no more than two club lengths away from the hazard in a spot equidistant from the flagstick on the other side of the hazard (one-stroke penalty).

To make a proper drop, hold the ball at arm's length away from your body and level with your shoulder, and then release it to the ground.

## WHITE STAKES

A white stake indicates out of bounds or areas from which you are not allowed to hit a ball. Courses also use other property lines, such as a fence, to indicate out of bounds. If your ball crosses into an area marked by white stakes, you must go back to the spot from which you originally hit and play another ball, taking a one-stroke penalty.

If you fear that you may not be able to find your ball after hitting it—for example, if you hit a slice into a wooded area—hit another ball (called a *provisional ball*) so that you don't have to walk all the way back to the original spot if your first ball doesn't turn up. Let your playing partners know that you are hitting a provisional ball.

*CONTINUED ON NEXT PAGE*

## Lost and Found

### SEARCHING FOR A LOST BALL

According to the official rules, you are entitled to search for a lost ball for five minutes. If you don't find it within that time frame, you must return to the spot from which you originally hit it, play another ball, and record a penalty stroke. (Remember, if you hit a ball that you think might be difficult to find, hitting a provisional ball will save you a trip back to the original spot.) If you are playing a casual round and want to maintain a speedy pace of play, take a penalty stroke, drop a new ball as close as possible to where you think the ball was lost, and play from there.

### HITTING THE WRONG BALL

Always check before hitting to make sure that you are hitting your own ball. Marking the ball in some manner (such as with your initials, a pattern of dots, or a symbol like the one shown in the photo) will help ensure that you play the correct ball. In fact, it's good practice to mark all your balls with the same unique marking prior to beginning your round. Do it on both sides of the ball since you can't touch a ball in play except when it is on the green.

Hitting the wrong ball during competition incurs a two-stroke penalty in stroke play, or the loss of the hole in match play. You must go back and play your original ball if you have not yet completed the hole. In casual play, consider simply taking the penalty and moving on.

**On the Tee and on the Green**

## TEEING THE BALL WITHIN THE TEE MARKERS

When hitting from a tee box, you must tee the ball either even with the two tee markers or no more than two club lengths behind the markers. If you tee the ball in front of (as shown here), outside of, or more than two club lengths behind the markers, you will incur a two-stroke penalty in stroke play. In match play, there is no penalty, but your playing partner may require you to replay the shot.

## CLEANING THE "LINE OF PUTT"

You may use your hand or a towel to wipe away items on the "line of putt", including a leaf and a pebble. You may repair ball marks, but you cannot repair spike marks caused by golf shoes on that line.

*CONTINUED ON NEXT PAGE*

### TENDING THE FLAG

When all players have made it onto the putting surface, the flagstick is removed from the hole and placed off to the side where it won't get in the way of any errant putts. However, one player may "tend the flag," or hold the flagstick, while the other player putts. This is often done on a large green when the person putting has an especially long putt and/or can't see the hole clearly from where the ball lies.

If you tend the flag for another player, you must remove it if the ball is moving directly toward the hole. You cannot leave the flag in the hole if the other player is putting on the green; the person putting will incur a two-stroke penalty if the ball hits the pin while the flag is being tended. You can also tend the flag for someone putting from off the green.

## GROUNDING YOUR CLUB IN A BUNKER

You cannot *ground your club* (let it touch the sand prior to hitting the ball) when playing a bunker shot unless you are in a designated waste area (which is a large sandy area that is not maintained). You can hover the club directly behind the ball before such a shot, but grounding the club will incur a two-stroke penalty.

## BALL RESTING AGAINST A RAKE

If your ball lands up against a rake inside a bunker, you must carefully remove the rake. If the ball moves when you move the rake, you must return it to its original spot.

## OBJECTS IN A BUNKER

You may remove any artificial objects (such as plastic cups) that you find in a bunker affecting your ball or stance. However, you cannot move any natural objects (such as leaves) if they are near or touching the ball.

*CONTINUED ON NEXT PAGE*

## Obstructions

## OBJECTS AFFECTING YOUR STANCE

If an object such as a storm drain or paved cart path interferes with your stance or swing, you are allowed to seek relief. Find the nearest point away from the obstacle to drop the ball, but make sure that you do not drop the ball any closer to the hole.

## OBJECTS AFFECTING THE BALL

If your ball is in the fairway or rough, you may remove a leaf or twig that is *covering* the ball. If doing so moves the ball, however, you incur a one-stroke penalty—so move the object very carefully! Remember that if the ball does move, you must place it back in its original position or you will incur another penalty stroke. If there is a leaf or twig *underneath* the ball, you must play the ball as it lies.

## UNPLAYABLE LIE

If you find yourself unable to make any type of shot because of an obstruction—for example, if your ball has landed against the trunk of a tree—you have three options, each of which requires one penalty stroke: 1) drop a ball within two club lengths of where it lies, but no closer to the hole, 2) drop a ball behind the spot where it lies, going as far backward as you want but staying on a line directly between the hole and that spot, or 3) play the ball from as near as possible to where you last hit it.

If you're playing in poor conditions, the lift (pick the ball up after marking its location), clean (wipe off dirt, grass, or moisture), and place (return to lie) rule may be used. Representatives of the course you are playing will determine whether this rule should be used. If you intend to post your score for handicap purposes, you must play by the rules declared by the course superintendent or head golf professional.

Every course provides a free scorecard for golfers to keep track of the strokes they take on each hole. The following categories receive their own space on a scorecard; you'll find a sample scorecard on the following page.

## Understanding the Scorecard

- **Hole number:** Shows the order in which holes are played. Usually one half of the scorecard shows holes 1–9 ("out"), while the other side shows holes 10–18 ("in"). This split enables you to fold the scorecard in half and place it in your pocket.

- **Yardage:** Represents the length of each hole. Scorecards often include multiple yardages for each hole, from longest (referred to as the "back tees" or "tips") to shortest ("forward tees"). Tees are assigned colors—usually black for the longest tees and red for the shortest. In the example on the following page, the course has four sets of tees.

- **Par:** Represents the number of strokes an accomplished player would need to finish each hole.

- **Handicap or Strokes:** Ranks the difficulty of each hole in relation to how a bogey golfer would play it compared to a scratch golfer. For example, the hole ranked number 1 in the Handicap or Strokes box would be the one that a bogey golfer would need the most help with when competing against a scratch golfer; the hole ranked 18th, the least. Keep in mind that these handicap strokes may differ from one set of tees to the next. For example, the number 1 handicap hole for men may not be the same as the number 1 hole for women.

  Handicap strokes (see page 159) are also applied using these rankings. If you are a 15 handicap, you receive one stroke each on the holes numbered 1–15 in this category. If your handicap is higher than 18, you apply one stroke to every hole and then add any remaining strokes to holes in order of handicap ranking. For example, if your handicap is 24, you would apply two strokes each to holes ranked 1–6 in handicap category; all others would receive one stroke. If you are playing against another player, you simply subtract the better player's handicap from the lesser player's handicap. For example, if you are a 24 handicap playing against a 10 handicap, you receive one stroke on the 14 holes ranked 1–14 in the Handicap or Strokes category.

- **Score box:** The area in which you record the number of strokes you took on each hole. There is usually enough room on a scorecard to track four players' scores.

Scorecards can be used to track more than just your score. You can also note other elements of play that will help you keep track of your progress. Examples include:

- The number of putts taken
- How many fairways you hit with your tee shots
- How many bunkers you landed in
- What clubs you used on each hole
- How many balls you lost and why (hit out-of-bounds, into the water, etc.)

By noting those statistics on each hole, you can study how you play a particular type of hole (for example, par-fives) and learn whether you need to change your overall playing strategy (such as by playing more conservatively or more aggressively).

*CONTINUED ON NEXT PAGE*

| HOLE | BLACK | BLUE | STROKES | | | | PAR | | STROKES | WHITE | RED |
|------|-------|------|---------|---|---|---|-----|---|---------|-------|-----|
| 1 | 538 | 513 | 7 | | | | 5 | | 1 | 491 | 469 |
| 2 | 389 | 378 | 9 | | | | 4 | | 11 | 356 | 340 |
| 3 | 177 | 159 | 17 | | | | 3 | | 17 | 144 | 126 |
| 4 | 435 | 418 | 1 | | | | 4 | | 5 | 393 | 367 |
| 5 | 500 | 489 | 11 | | | | 5 | | 7 | 471 | 417 |
| 6 | 392 | 375 | 15 | | | | 4 | | 13 | 341 | 315 |
| 7 | 217 | 206 | 13 | | | | 3 | | 15 | 173 | 161 |
| 8 | 528 | 512 | 3 | | | | 5 | | 3 | 482 | 464 |
| 9 | 440 | 410 | 5 | | | | 4 | | 9 | 347 | 276 |
| OUT | 3616 | 3457 | | | | | 37 | | | 3198 | 2935 |
| 10 | 390 | 362 | 10 | | | | 4 | | 12 | 337 | 314 |
| 11 | 197 | 175 | 16 | | | | 3 | | 16 | 158 | 125 |
| 12 | 601 | 579 | 2 | | | | 5 | | 2 | 553 | 526 |
| 13 | 417 | 375 | 4 | | | | 4 | | 10 | 354 | 318 |
| 14 | 157 | 138 | 18 | | | | 3 | | 18 | 121 | 89 |
| 15 | 521 | 502 | 6 | | | | 5 | | 8 | 485 | 444 |
| 16 | 359 | 337 | 12 | | | | 4 | | 4 | 307 | 289 |
| 17 | 247 | 191 | 14 | | | | 3 | | 14 | 170 | 150 |
| 18 | 414 | 394 | 8 | | | | 4 | | 6 | 356 | 325 |
| IN | 3303 | 3053 | | | | | 35 | | | 2841 | 2580 |
| TOT | 6919 | 6510 | | | | | 72 | | | 6039 | 5515 |
| HANDICAP | | | | | | | | | | | |
| NET SCORE | | | | | | | | | | | |

DATE        SCORER        ATTEST

## Calculating Your Handicap

Although some golfers consider their swing (or perhaps, jokingly, their playing partner) their handicap, they would be wrong, technically speaking. A course handicap is a number that helps level the playing field when you compete against a better or worse player with a lower or higher handicap. It's a great way to measure your improvement as a golfer no matter what level of player you are. How that number gets calculated, though, is a bit complicated.

To get a course handicap, you first need to establish a USGA Handicap Index. To do so, you must be a member of a golf club (that doesn't mean you must join a private club—many public courses have clubs specifically for handicap purposes) and submit your scores for the rounds you play via a computer at the course.

The Handicap Index is based on the average of your ten best rounds from the last 20 rounds you have played. It is not based on your ten best scores alone, though, because the rating and slope of each course you play are factored into the calculation as well. You will receive a handicap card from the USGA that shows those scores and your handicap index (as well as your home course handicap).

Your Handicap Index is then converted into a Course Handicap for each course you play. To find the latter number, look for a Handicap Conversion Chart (there is a separate one for each set of tees) posted at the course. There is no need to do any calculating when you look at the table because it shows the course handicap for any Handicap Index. The Handicap Indexes have a decimal point, so it gives a range; if your index is 10.6 and it shows that indexes between 10.2 and 11.0 have a Course Handicap of 12 from the set of tees you will be playing from, then your course handicap is 12.

Keep in mind that your Course Handicap, which will vary from course to course, is just an indication of your potential playing ability. Just because you may be playing a par-72 course with a 15 handicap doesn't mean that you will shoot an 87 on that course every time. It's more likely that your scores will be above that, not an average of what you actually shoot.

If you want to calculate your Handicap Index on your own, here's how:

1 Subtract the course rating (usually found on the scorecard) from your score.

2 Multiply that number by 113 and divide that result by the slope rating (usually found on the scorecard).

3 Multiply by 0.96 to get what's called a *differential.*

4 Average the best ten differentials of your last 20 rounds to determine your Handicap Index.

### FACT

In a golf tournament, players sign their scorecards before turning them in to the tournament officials. Signing an incorrect scorecard can lead to a stroke penalty or disqualification. The most famous example of this in professional golf came at the 1968 Masters, when Roberto De Vicenzo signed a scorecard containing an incorrect score on the 17th hole in the final round. The mistake meant that De Vicenzo wound up losing the tournament to Bob Goalby by one stroke. Always double-check your scores before signing the scorecard!

In addition to the official rules, there is proper golf etiquette to keep in mind while playing. This section describes numerous situations you should know about.

## ORDER OF PLAY

On the first tee, you need to choose who in your group will play first. That can be decided randomly; it is often done by throwing a tee into the air—whomever it points to goes first and so on until each person in the group has been assigned a spot in the order.

The person who finishes with the lowest score on the first hole tees off first on the second hole. That person maintains teeing ground "honors" until someone else shoots a lower score on a hole.

As you play, the person farthest from the hole plays first. When on the green, you can *putt out* (or continue to putt until the ball makes it into the hole) if you are not in someone else's putting line and you get permission to do so from the other players. Otherwise, each person takes turns putting in order of who is farthest from the hole.

In all situations, always be ready to hit your shot as soon as the other players are done with their shots. Do not wait until another player hits to plan your shot and choose the right club. And don't make noise while other players are hitting!

## FAQ

### What's a mulligan?

A mulligan occurs when a player is unhappy with the outcome of a shot (usually a tee shot) and then repeats the same shot without taking a penalty stroke. This unofficial safety net is not recognized by the rules of golf; you can never take a mulligan during any official round. People usually play better when no one in the group takes a mulligan, and play tends to go quicker. For beginners, though, a mulligan can be considered a do-over.

## PACE OF PLAY

Maintaining an efficient pace of play is important on every course. On most courses, the average time to play 18 holes is four hours and 15 minutes. To avoid slow play, keep these points in mind:

- Always bring an extra club for the situation when walking to your ball.
- Plan your shot while others are hitting, and be ready to hit when it's your turn.
- Write your score down on the next tee instead of on the green you just finished playing.
- Walk briskly throughout the round.
- If you bring a club other than your putter to the green (such as a wedge), place it on or near the flagstick—never off in the rough where it could be forgotten.
- Keep an eye on your ball and that of your playing partner; pick a tree, a bush, or another point to help you locate the ball you just hit.
- Hit an extra ball, known as a provisional ball, if you think your first shot may result in a lost ball.
- If the hole in front of you is open (that is, no one is playing on it) and the group behind you is waiting, let them play through if their group is smaller than yours. Your foursome should then try to maintain your position just behind the group in front of you.

- In casual play, if the number of strokes you have taken on a hole is double the par of that hole (for example, you have taken eight shots on a par-four), pick up your ball and move on to the next hole.
- Putt out. Marking your ball on the green and then re-marking it when it's your turn to hit takes a lot of time. Go ahead and finish, as long as you don't stand in someone else's line.

## CART PATHS

If you are using a cart, always follow the signs on the course indicating where you can and cannot go. If you see signs indicating "Cart Paths Only," you can't drive the cart anywhere other than on those paths. A sign stating "Cart 90 Degrees Only" means that while you can drive the cart on the fairway, it must be at a 90-degree angle to the direction of the fairway at any given point. Never drive a cart on a tee box or green.

***CONTINUED ON NEXT PAGE***

## REPLACING DIVOTS

Always replace the divot you leave after hitting a tee shot or fairway shot. Find the piece of grass that's likely in front of where you hit from and place it back in the bare spot you created. Today, most carts come with a container full of a mixture of sand and grass seed; simply spread the mixture over the divot and smooth it out.

## RAKING THE SAND AFTER A BUNKER SHOT

Always rake the sand in a bunker as neatly as possible after you have a hit a shot. Rake both the spot from which you hit the ball and any footprints you have made. Take note of where the rakes are placed and then return the rake you used to the same spot after you have finished raking the sand. Some courses keep the rakes inside the bunkers, while others place them just outside the bunkers.

## REPAIRING BALL MARKS ON THE GREEN

Always repair any mark your ball may have made when landing on the green. Insert the divot repair tool into the ground around the edge of the mark and gently push toward the center of the mark. While you're at it, be a good Samaritan and fix ball marks made by other players, too.

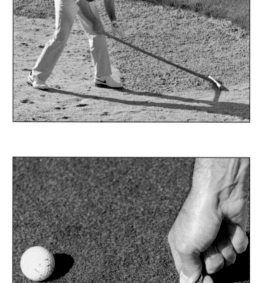

## MARKING YOUR BALL ON THE GREEN

Always mark your ball on the green when playing with others so that your ball does not block another player's path to the hole. If your mark is in another person's path, you can move the mark one putter clubhead length to the left or right of the original spot. Before you putt, return the ball to its original spot.

## STEERING CLEAR OF OTHERS' PUTTING LINES

A putting line on the green is the path on which a player intends to putt the ball. Never step on the putting line of another player, and do not stand behind or in front of another player on that line. If the person putting can see your foot while he or she is in position to hit the ball, then you are too close. Remember to be still and quiet while others are putting.

In addition to *stroke play* (whoever finishes with the fewest strokes wins) or *match play* (where a hole is either won or halved), you can play or use numerous other games and scoring formats on the course. Besides providing another competitive outlet, each game can help you stay involved in your round no matter how well or poorly you're playing. And they're fun!

- **Alternate Shot:** In this format, two players form a team and hit alternate shots on each hole: If Player A hits the tee shot, Player B hits the next shot, and so on.
- **Best Ball:** A popular outing format in which all players in a foursome play their own ball, with the lowest score (or "best ball") counting as the team's score for that hole.
- **Bingo Bango Bongo:** A format that puts separate values on a player's long game, short game, and putting. On each hole, 3 points are available to win: The first point goes to the player who reaches the green in the fewest strokes; the second point goes to the player who is closest to the pin after everyone is on the green; and the final point is awarded to the player who gets the ball into the hole in the fewest strokes overall.
- **Callaway:** You may play in an event in which the Callaway scoring system is used. This system helps determine net scores for players without an established handicap and helps equalize the playing field for various skill levels.
- **Four Ball:** Used when playing in a foursome, this format pits the best ball (lowest score) of one twosome against the best ball of the other twosome.
- **Nassau:** This form of match play betting involves separate wagers on the front nine score, the back nine score, and the overall result of the match. For example, if Player A is two up through nine holes, he or she wins the front nine. If Player A then loses the back nine one down, he or she loses the wager for that nine. The overall score has Player A winning one up over 18 holes.
- **Points:** This game involves the awarding of points to players on each hole depending on their scores. For example, if you're playing in a threesome, 9 points could be available on every hole; the best score gets 5 points, the second best gets 3 points, and the third best gets 1 point. If all players get the same score for the hole, each one gets 3 points.
- **Sandies/Greenies:** Also referred to as "garbage"; points are awarded for sandies (when a player takes one shot out of a bunker and then one putt on the green—in some versions, the putt has to be for par) and greenies, awarded to the closest player to the pin on a hole (usually only on par-threes). The player with the most points in each of those categories, or a combined total, wins.
- **Scramble:** The most frequently used format for outings has all players in the group hit tee shots. The best drive of the group is then selected, and all players hit from that point; the best of those shots is selected, and all players hit from there. This process continues until the ball is in the hole. Usually a minimum of three drives from each player in the group must be used within 18 holes.
- **Shamble:** In this fun outing format, all players hit tee shots and the best is picked; then all players play their own balls from that point into the hole.
- **Skins:** This format puts a prize ("skin") on each hole, with the lowest score winning the skin. If there is no single lowest score, that skin carries over to the next hole, and so on. Whoever ends up with the most skins at the end of the round wins the predetermined reward. It's a great game for beginners because each hole is its own separate match.
- **Stableford:** In this format, point values are assigned to each type of score per hole (eagle, birdie, par, bogey, etc.). Each player accumulates points based on how well he or she does relative to par. The player with the most points at the end of the round wins.
- **Wolf:** Wolf is typically a three-player game in which players alternate who plays against the others on each hole. On each tee, a designated player chooses who his or her partner will be for the hole, with the better ball (or lowest score) of those two players matched up against the best ball of the remaining player in the group.

Golf is often used for corporate and charity outings, many of which are played at private clubs. Some involve clinics in the morning followed by golf in the afternoon; others are solely rounds of golf. An invitation to such an event can strike fear in the heart of an inexperienced player, but you really shouldn't pass up the opportunity. Most events are played using the scramble format (see page 164), which means that you are part of a team—usually a foursome. This format is more relaxed than playing your own ball and counting every stroke. However, you should be aware of some essential guidelines if you are a guest at an outing, and keep some important things in mind if you are hosting a friend or colleague at your local course or a private club.

## HOW TO BE A GOOD GUEST

- Follow the appropriate dress code (many private clubs do not allow players to wear shorts, for example).
- Ask your host or call the club to find out about the tipping policy. If allowed, consider tipping for services rendered; potential recipients include locker room attendants, outside service staff (the people who carry your clubs to and from your car or clean the clubs after you play), the starter, caddies, and the beverage cart person.
- Arrive on time or be slightly early. You should be prepared to make your first swing at tee time.
- Because many outings involve a shotgun start, where foursomes begin play simultaneously on different holes around the course, find out which hole your group is starting on.
- Don't swear or throw clubs, and avoid temper tantrums no matter how frustrated you may be with your game. Remember that as a guest, you are a reflection of the member who is hosting you.
- If you are really struggling on a hole, pick up your ball and prepare for the next hole.
- Follow all posted rules on and off the course (keep your cart on the cart path, refrain from using your cell phone, etc.).
- Always offer to pay for your round.
- Treat the staff politely.
- Compliment your host about the day, the club, and the course.
- After an official outing, a cocktail hour and/or dinner is usually held, so bring a change of clothes. Find out ahead of time whether more formal attire is required.

## HOW TO BE A GRACIOUS HOST

- Give your guest all the appropriate information beforehand: explain the rules and dress code, designate a time of arrival and a place to meet, offer directions, and point out the practice facilities.
- Choose appropriate players for a foursome based on playing skills and personalities.
- Arrive early to greet your guest as he or she arrives.
- Take care of confirming the start time and paying for green fees.
- If the outing is using a shotgun start, make sure that your guest knows which hole to begin on.
- Buy a souvenir (such as a hat or logo golf balls) for your guest.
- If you are a member, arrange for a locker that your guest can use for the day.
- Make your guest comfortable; keep it positive on the course, and focus on your guest rather than on your own game.
- If your guest is not playing well, suggest a different format that would be more fun.
- Let faster groups play through.
- Buy a post-round refreshment for your guest.

# chapter 10

# Troubleshooting and Tricky Shots

If golf were an easy game, we would all be highly paid professionals playing for buckets of prize money. Unfortunately, though, it isn't easy. So much of your body is involved in the golf swing—your hands, your arms, your legs, your shoulders, and, last but not least, your brain—that, for beginners, making a swing that results in a straight shot can be considered a small miracle. Your odds of repeating that result will improve as you gain experience, but things will go wrong sometimes, largely because the path that your club follows during the swing is off.

Hitting slice after slice, or popping the ball up into the air a few times in a row, gets frustrating quickly. Those beautiful trees lining the fairways? Not so nice when your ball is directly underneath some overhanging branches that limit your swing. Those perfectly manicured fairways? They look great until your ball comes to a stop on an uneven lie.

With the proper techniques, however, you can handle tricky situations like these successfully. This chapter discusses ways to tackle troublesome shots and situations on the course, along with some drills that will help prevent your swing from going wrong in the first place.

Most golfers play right-handed, and most of them slice the ball. That doesn't mean that they cut it into pieces—*slice* is the name for a shot that curves dramatically from left to right (not be confused with a fade, which also curves from left to right, but on purpose and in a controlled manner; or a push, where the ball moves directly to the right immediately after being hit).

## What Causes a Slice

A slice is caused by an open clubface coming across the ball—glancing against it instead of striking it squarely—which makes the ball peel out to the right. You may have been aiming straight out at the target (represented by the bottom board in the photo), but the club is coming down across the ball and heading too far to the left of the target, as represented by the top board in the photo.

## FAQ

**Can I use a slice to my advantage?**

Only in very limited situations can a slice be useful. For instance, if you're hitting to a fairway that bends severely to the right, a slice can curve around that bend thanks to its flight path. In virtually every other situation, though, a slice will do you more harm than good. Better to work on fixing it than to try working around it!

## Shoulders

A major problem that causes slicing is allowing your shoulders to turn too quickly through the downswing, which can make it difficult to square the clubface at impact. To slow them down, try this drill.

Lay a board (or a club) down on the ground pointing toward a target. Assume your stance in front of the board, and extend your left arm to hold the top of your driver, which should rest on the other side of the board. Hold a second club in your right hand, as if to hit a ball.

Slowly swing the club in your right hand through the opening between your body and the board on the ground while keeping your left hand on top of the driver in front of you. This drill helps slow the rotation of your shoulders during the swing, which promotes a square clubface at impact and reduces the likelihood of a swing that comes across the ball.

***CONTINUED ON NEXT PAGE***

## Hands

If your hands are not in the proper position during the swing, the chances of your clubface being square at impact are slim—and that's when a slice can happen. Here's a drill you can do to get a feel for the correct position of your left hand.

Hold a ball in your left hand while your right hand rests on top of a club. Move your left hand through a regular swing motion while holding onto the ball.

As you take your left hand through the swing motion, you should see half of the ball facing up at the point of impact. When you get to the follow-through position (your left palm should be facing up), you should see the entire ball, since your hands will have rolled over during the swing. Doing this drill helps you release (or roll over) your hands through the swing, enabling you to square the clubface and providing more power when you strike the ball. If you don't release your hands, the clubhead won't turn over properly, and you may find yourself slicing the ball.

Next, put a club in your hand and make a partial swing. Try to re-create the feeling and motion you experienced when the ball was in your left hand.

**Note:** *The position of the clubhead in the photo is exaggerated to emphasize the left hand position. Ideally, the toe of the club would be pointing up in the air.*

Do this drill as often as possible on the course, including while you wait for other players to tee off or while awaiting your turn on the fairway.

## Miss the Bucket

If you're slicing shots to the right or pulling the ball to the left, you are swinging the club too far outside to inside on the downswing. If the club continues on that path, you will pull the ball to the left. If you try to adjust the position of the club with your hands, you will open the clubface and cut across the ball, leading to a slice.

The buckets you see on driving ranges can do more than just hold practice balls. You can use one to work on building the proper swing path. Place a bucket (ideally an empty one) just ahead of your front foot, between yourself and the ball. Take a swing and try to avoid hitting the bucket. Doing so encourages you to swing from inside to square to outside—an exaggeration of the proper swing path (inside to square to inside), but useful to help correct the outside-to-inside path that causes a slice.

A hook is the opposite of a slice—and equally undesirable. A hooked ball curves dramatically from right to left (not to be confused with a draw, which also moves from left to right, but on purpose and in a controlled manner; or a pull, where the ball moves directly to the left immediately after being struck).

## What Causes a Hook

A hooked shot happens either when the clubhead gets ahead of your hands at impact, causing the clubface to hit the ball in a closed position, or the swing path of the club is excessively inside to outside. Remember, your goal is for the club to travel on an inside-to-square-to-inside swing path.

### FAQ

**Can I use a hook to my advantage?**
A hook can be useful, but only in limited situations. For example, if you're playing a hole with a fairway that bends severely to the left, a hook can bend around the fairway with its exaggerated flight path. In virtually every other situation, though, a hooked shot will do you more harm than good. Try working on some drills that will help you reduce your chances of hooking the ball, as described on the following pages.

## Miss the Bucket

If you're pushing the ball out to the right or hooking shots to the left, you are probably moving on an inside-to-outside path during the downswing instead of on an inside-to-square-to-inside path. If the clubface stays square to that path, you will hit a push shot. If you try to adjust the position of the club with your hands, you will likely turn the clubhead over at impact and hook the ball left.

To work on correcting your swing path, grab a bucket from the driving range. Place the bucket (either empty or full of practice balls) just behind your back foot and between yourself and the ball.

Then take a swing, making sure that your club misses the bucket on the downswing.

*CONTINUED ON NEXT PAGE*

During the downswing, keep the club out in front of the bucket. This motion exaggerates what a proper swing should feel like, but doing so will help you correct the problem. You want to feel your hips open up to the target, with your hands and the clubhead following to the left (or inside) after you hit the ball.

When you reach the finish position, the bottom of your back foot should be turned up and facing the bucket.

**At Impact**

In an ideal swing, the clubhead compresses squarely against the back of the ball at impact. To make this happen, the shaft of the club must be leaning slightly forward so that your hands line up with the ball before the clubhead gets to the same position.

To practice the feeling of a square clubface at impact, place the back end of a two-by-four where the ball would normally be. Point the board toward a target.

Set up with the clubhead touching the end of the board. Then assume the impact position: Your hips should be starting to open up toward the target, your hands should be ahead of the clubhead, and your left wrist should be flat. Slowly push the board toward the target. Repeat this process a few times; then replace the board with a ball and hit some half-shots to achieve the same feeling. Doing so will help you break the habit of getting the clubhead ahead of your hands, which results in hooked shots.

If your hands are behind the clubhead at impact, the clubhead will start to rise up the board instead of feeling like it is going down into the ground. That can result in a closed clubface, which can lead to hooked shots. You will also feel your weight hanging back on your right side instead of having moved to your left side. If a ball were there, you might hit the upper half of the ball, which could lead to a topped and/or hooked shot.

**TIP**

**Square the Clubhead**
Hooked shots can also be caused by a grip (see Chapter 3) that is too strong in either hand. A strong grip promotes a closed clubface (useful for hitting a draw, but also the cause of a hook) and more active hands, which enable you to release the club sooner during the downswing. The catch is that you need a lot of lateral leg drive to counterbalance that early release. In this situation, a more neutral grip will help you square the clubface and likely reduce the number of hooked shots you hit.

# Avoid Hitting Fat Shots

Hitting the ball fat means that the clubhead hits the ground before making contact with the ball resulting in a big divot and much less distance than you expected. This problem is caused by the club swinging on an inside-to-outside path (see page 72) and failing to hit the ball squarely, or a poor weight transfer from your back foot to your front foot.

## Correct Your Weight Shift

A proper weight shift will help prevent not only fat shots, but weak slices and dramatic hooks as well. Many golfers allow their weight to move to the outside of the right foot during the backswing, making it more difficult to shift it forward during the downswing. The end result is an off-balance swing, because the weight never moves to the front foot.

To practice your weight shift, place a ball underneath the outside of your back foot and take a normal swing, making sure not to lose your balance. If your back foot starts to wobble, apply more pressure to the inside of your right foot.

This drill encourages you to keep your weight in the correct place during the backswing and the downswing, causing you to finish properly with your weight on the front leg.

## Learn from the Placement of Your Divots

Your divots are valuable learning tools that can help you eliminate fat shots. To create a proper divot, you need to hit the ball first and then the turf.

To see whether you're hitting the ground in the proper position, draw a line perpendicular to your target and place a ball directly on the line, or put a tee next to the ball. After hitting the ball, take a look at the divot you created. If the divot starts behind the line or tee, you're hitting the ground before hitting the ball—not good. The divot should be in front of that line, as shown here. (The ball in the photo is just below where it would have been prior to being hit.)

The width of your divot says a lot, too. It should be as wide as the face of the club you used. A narrower divot indicates that your clubface was not square to the target at impact.

## TIP

Many people who hook the ball have an overactive lower body. Their legs drive laterally toward the target during the downswing, with both knees staying flexed. This lateral leg drive keeps the club traveling down the target line too long after impact rather than coming back around to the inside. Focus on straightening your left leg at impact. Feel as though you are posting up onto the left leg, with your weight going into your left heel. This will help your hips open up faster and enable the club to swing back to the inside after the ball is hit.

# Avoid Hitting Thin or Topping

Tense arms that pull in toward your body at impact, along with a far too active lower body (moving your weight forward too quickly or changing your posture during the swing), can lead to thin or topped shots. Either action positions the club just high enough that it hits the middle (thin) or top (topped) of the ball, resulting in a line drive (thin) that can't be controlled or a ball that hits the ground immediately rather than going up into the air (topped). These drills will help you fix these nasty problems.

## Feet Together

To avoid hitting thin or topping, try a drill where you take half-swings with your feet together. Doing so will help you learn how to swing your arms and the clubhead freely back to the ball without your lower body interfering. Try to keep your arms as relaxed as possible during the half-swing so that they can remain extended through impact.

Place a tee in the ground where your ball would normally be. Put a second tee an inch or two in front of the other, with both lined up in the direction of a target.

Stand with your feet together and take a half-swing to feel the sensation of the clubhead turning over while your lower body stays quiet. Doing so will slow down your hip rotation during the swing and help you reach a square clubhead position at impact.

Keeping your feet together makes it harder for your hips to open toward the target too soon, and makes it harder for your shoulders to rotate too quickly. Hitting both tees also improves your ability to take a proper divot by hitting down and through where the ball would be.

Practice this drill in three phases:

- First, try to clip both tees out of the ground to get "longer" at impact.
- Then pick a spot on the ground and practice hitting it. Try to create a divot in front of the spot, not behind it.
- Finally, put a ball down and try to hit the ball first and then the ground. Pretend that there is a tee under the ball, and swing as if you were trying to hit the imaginary tee.

**FACT**

You may hear other golfers use the phrase "hit it thin to win." This phrase refers to the rare situation in which a thin shot actually finishes near the intended target. That result is almost always a fluke; you want to eliminate thin or topped shots from your game as much as possible.

# Stop Hitting Pop-Ups

If your shots are popping straight up into the air after impact, your club is approaching the ball at too steep an angle and with a face that is too open. You are likely taking the club up into the air and then straight down to the ball at a steep angle. The solution is to create a flatter, more sweeping arc and a square clubface at impact—think of a U-shaped swing rather than a V-shaped swing.

## High Tee

To promote a flatter swing and solid contact, especially with long irons and hybrids, tee a ball up as high as you can. Only a flatter swing will be able to make solid contact with a ball in this position; if your swing is still too steep, you will hit the tee, and the ball will go straight up into the air. You will also be reminded of the importance of squaring the clubface through impact. If the ball flies high and right, then your clubface is still open.

### TIP

Put another ball an inch or two behind the ball you want to hit and place the club between the two balls. As start your backswing, try to push the second ball backward with the clubhead. Doing so helps prevent an early wrist cock and decreases any potential chopping motion in your swing, thereby creating a flatter, U-shaped swing.

If your shots are staying low to the ground and not going in the direction you're aiming (known as a line drive or "skulled" shot), the club's leading edge—or the very bottom of the clubface—is hitting the middle of the ball, instead of the clubface itself hitting the ball. This problem can be caused by sliding your head past the ball prior to impact. That means your upper body is beating your lower body to the ball.

**TIP**

Want another visual image to remind you of remaining steady and keeping your head behind the ball? Imagine an iron a few inches from the side of your head. You wouldn't want your head to make contact with a hot iron, would you?

# Know Your Divots

A divot is more than just a piece of turf that you knock into the air with your club. The direction of each divot can tell you a lot about the swing you just made.

## Learn from the Angle of Your Divots

For this drill, lay a board on the ground, pointing toward your target. Place a ball between yourself and the board and take a shot.

If your divot is pointing right, toward the target line (indicated by the white board in the photo), you have pushed the ball to the right or hooked the ball to the left.

If your divot is pointing left, away from the target line, you have pulled your shot to the left or sliced your shot to the right.

## TIP

In either situation, it's possible that your swing isn't the problem, especially if you don't have a board to guide you. Your stance may have been pointing right or left of the target when you set up for the shot, eliminating any chance you had of hitting the ball where you wanted it to go. Know your target line so that you can check your divot in relation to how you set up for the shot. A simple drill is to lay a club down just beyond the ball, pointed along the path you want the ball to travel. Then take a swing and see if your divot is in line with the club on the ground.

Not every golfer replaces the divots they create in the fairway (but you always should!). That means your ball may occasionally wind up on a patch of dirt—a lie that often produces a thin shot.

## Dirt, Not Grass

In this situation, you need to make sure that you feel centered in your stance. It's critical to keep your lower body stable and not shift your weight much, if at all, during the swing.

First, position the ball toward the back of your stance. Doing so will help you hit the ball with a descending blow. Then get your hands slightly ahead of the ball, weight favoring your left side, and aim slightly left of your target. This helps you create an outside-to-inside swing path—more of a V-shaped swing than the usually preferable U-shaped swing. You want to come down at the ball at a steeper angle so that the clubhead doesn't get caught in the turf on the back edge of the divot. You also want to square the clubface to the ball's intended flight path.

As usual, your goal is to hit the ball first, not the ground. (Someone already did that for you if you're in a divot!) Also, the clubhead should reach the ball while it's still moving downward, and not on the upswing.

### TIP

No golfer purposely aims to hit the ball into a divot, and no one leaves a divot behind hoping that someone will land in it. It's all part of playing golf—an unlucky position that happens to everyone eventually if they play often enough. Don't focus so much on the poor lie; instead, try to maintain a positive attitude and challenge yourself to execute the shot as best you can. Then move on to the next shot.

# Hit from Up Against the Collar

Occasionally, you may find your ball in an unusual situation around the green—up against the collar, where the fringe of the putting surface meets the rough. You can use your putter for this shot, but you must hit the ball with a descending blow (more of a V-shaped swing) rather than the sweeping motion you would normally use for a putt (a U-shaped swing). With a regular swing, you could miss the ball entirely since it is almost hidden by the grass.

## Strike the Ball with a Descending Blow

Keep your hands ahead of the clubhead throughout this swing. The length of your backswing depends on the distance you're trying to cover. Keep in mind that the ball will roll more than usual and will often jump forward immediately after impact since the grass that comes between the clubface and the ball will eliminate any backspin.

Because you're hitting down on the ball, this shot doesn't require as much of a backswing. However, you should hinge your wrists immediately during the backswing and focus your eyes on the top of the ball. Your hands and arms should be very relaxed, with your weight shifted slightly left. The impact you want to make with the ball is more of a gentle tap than a hard punch.

Sooner or later, your ball will wind up under a tree whose low branches will impair your swing. In this situation, your main goal is simply to hit the ball to a spot from which you can then swing comfortably. Don't try for too much—all you want is to get yourself in position for the next shot.

## Get Out of There!

Because the tree branches will limit the length of your swing, you will need to make some adjustments to your grip and stance. Choke down on the club's grip and position the ball toward your back foot. This will help produce a lower-trajectory shot with more roll, helping you compensate for the abbreviated swing you will make. Your weight should be slightly forward toward your front foot.

Take some practice swings, shortening your backswing to the point where the tree branches do not interfere.

Keep your body down and through the actual swing, matching the length of your follow-through to the length of your backswing. If you lift your body at impact, you will hit a thin shot.

# Hit Out of Deep Rough

Just off the fairways at many golf courses lies evil grass known as deep rough. Balls hit into this area quickly disappear from view, nestling themselves into the tall, gnarly grass to create a difficult lie for your next shot. This rough is often thick enough to twist the club's hosel and close the clubface, producing off-target shots.

Since the grass in the deep rough will come between the ball and the clubface, you have little control over where the ball might go, and the club can put little spin on the ball. This decreases accuracy and makes the ball hard to stop when it does land—a real problem if you're trying to land the ball on the green. Your goal in this situation is simply to advance the ball to a place where you will have a better lie and therefore will be able to take a more productive swing.

To combat the thick rough, set up just left of your target and open up the clubface slightly. Doing so helps offset the grass pulling the clubface left and enables the club to cut through the grass better. Choke down on the club a few inches from the end, and increase your grip pressure so that you can keep hold of the club as it cuts through the rough.

You want to use an outside-to-inside swing (see page 73) path to create the steeper angle needed to hit the ball first and not the grass behind the ball. This path will correspond to your stance, which should be slightly left of your target. In effect, you will be swinging along the line created by your feet.

## TIP

When faced with a shot from deep rough, examine the grass. If the grass is growing in the direction of the hole, use a more lofted club, because it will slide through the grass easier, and the grass will not resist the clubhead as much. If the grass is growing away from the target, it will offer more resistance. Think more defensively in this situation and consider laying up; you're usually better off hitting a wedge than trying to muscle a club through deep rough that is working against you.

When your ball ends up on a sidehill lie, it is positioned either above or below your feet. Either way, the ball not being level with your feet will directly impact your stance, alignment, and swing and the direction of your shot. Since it's rare that you are able to practice hitting from such a lie, understanding the adjustments you need to make will make this seemingly difficult shot a bit easier to play.

## When the Ball Is Above Your Feet

When the ball is positioned above your feet, you need to make the following adjustments:

- Use a more lofted club than you normally would for the yardage you are trying to hit, because this lie produces a right-to-left draw shot that will roll farther than a typical shot. For example, if you would normally hit a 6-iron, opt for a 7-iron instead.

- Aim to the right of your target, since the uphill slope will make your shot move to the left.

- Position the ball more toward your back foot when you take your stance.

- Stand tall when addressing the ball, and keep your weight on the balls of your feet to help maintain balance through the swing.

- Grip down on the club. How far down depends on the severity of the lie—the steeper the incline, the farther down you should grip.

  Take a practice swing and hit the ground to find out how far you need to bend over and how much to grip down on the club.

- Make a flatter swing, with your arms lower than usual at the top of the backswing. This type of swing produces draws and the potential for hitting a fat shot. (That's why you place the ball back in your stance and aim right of your target.)

*CONTINUED ON NEXT PAGE*

## When the Ball Is Below Your Feet

This is the most difficult lie to play from because it has the greatest potential for a topped shot (where the clubface hits the top of the ball). When the ball is positioned below your feet, you need to make the following adjustments:

- Use a less lofted club than you normally would for the yardage you are trying to hit, because this lie puts a side spin on the ball that produces less roll. For example, if you would normally hit a 9-iron, try an 8-iron instead.

- Aim to the left of your target, since the downward slope will produce a fade-shaped shot that moves from left to right.

- Where you place the ball in your stance depends on which club you are using. For an 8-iron through sand wedge, place it in the middle; for a fairway wood, place it just left of center.

  Take a practice swing first and hit the ground to find out where the swing will bottom out—this will help ensure that you make good contact with the ball.

- Widen your stance and keep your weight back toward your heels to maintain balance throughout the swing.

- Grip the club as close to the end as you can.

When the ball is below your feet, your swing should be more upright than usual. Your arms and hands go up a little higher than normal during the backswing, and then back down to the ball. This more upright swing makes it easier to hit down on the ball and make a divot. It can also lead to an open clubface, which is why you want to aim left of the target.

# Hit Off a Downhill Lie

Your ball may come to rest in a downhill lie. Because the ground you're standing on will be sloping downward, you will have to alter your normal stance, alignment, and swing, plus take into account the distance a shot from this lie will travel.

## Make Adjustments for a Downhill Lie

When the ball is positioned on a downhill lie, you need to make the following adjustments:

- Stand with your shoulders and hips parallel to the downward slope; your right shoulder will naturally be higher than your left shoulder.

You don't want to keep your shoulders level or tilt them in the opposite direction of the slope. If you do so, you will likely lose your balance during the swing. You might also top the ball, since your shoulders won't be level with the downhill slope and the club might bottom out early, hitting the top of the ball on the upswing instead of catching it cleanly.

- Position the ball more toward your back foot.
- Balls hit off a downhill slope tend to go right, so aim to the left of your target.
- To help increase the trajectory of the ball, use a more lofted club than you normally would for the distance.
- Expect the ball to roll farther than normal because the ball will fly lower than normal from this lie. Be sure to pick a landing area short of your intended target to allow for the extra roll.
- Grip down on the club.
- Take a limited backswing—approximately three-quarters of a full backswing. Feel as if you are swinging the club up the hill on the backswing and down the slope on the downswing.

# Hit Off an Uphill Lie

Getting the ball into the air is usually not a problem from an uphill lie. But because the ground you're standing on is sloping upward, you will need to change your stance, alignment, and swing accordingly. You also need to consider the distance a shot travels when it is hit uphill.

## Make Adjustments for an Uphill Lie

When the ball is positioned on an uphill lie, you need to make the following adjustments:

- Stand with your shoulders and hips parallel to the upward slope; your left shoulder will naturally be higher than your right shoulder.

You don't want to keep your shoulders level or tilt them in the opposite direction of the slope. If you do so, you will likely lose your balance during the swing, and the club might hit the ground first, likely causing a fat shot.

- Position the ball more toward your front foot.

- Balls hit off an uphill slope tend to go left, so aim to the right of your target. That happens because it's difficult to turn the lower body properly on this type of lie (gravity causes you to lean back), therefore your arms and hands get ahead of your body earlier than normal, which causes the clubface to close.

- Use a less lofted club than you normally would for the distance; the ball will naturally fly higher because of the uphill slope.

- Grip down on the club.

- Feel as if you are swinging along the slope—don't hit into it. Your backswing should feel like it is going down the slope, while your downswing is moving up it.

- When judging the distance you have to hit the ball in this situation, expect a higher trajectory and less roll. To adjust for that, be sure to pick a landing area close to your target.

chapter **11**

# Improving Your Game

There are only two ways to get better at golf: take lessons from an experienced instructor and then practice, practice, practice. This chapter discusses the value of lessons, the types of lessons you can take, who to take them from, the overall goals and expectations you should have, and various ways you can practice with a purpose.

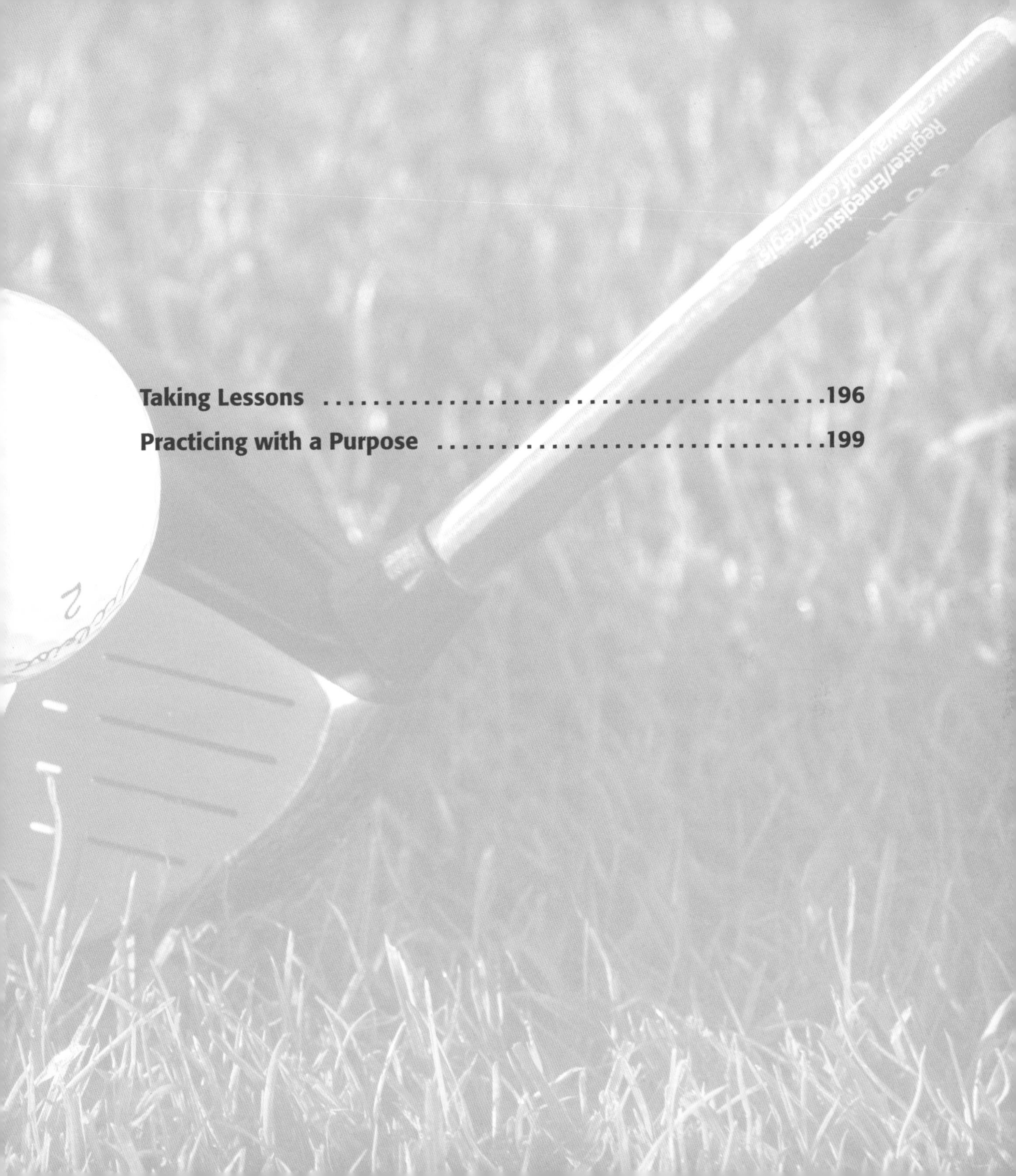

The golf swing—and the game itself—has so many facets that no one can learn them all effectively on their own. Everyone needs help, even champions like Tiger Woods and Annika Sorenstam. Fortunately, there are trained instructors who work with golfers at all levels. This section explains the various issues you must know about when it comes to taking lessons.

## HOW TO FIND AN INSTRUCTOR

There is no shortage of people out there who think they can help you with your golf game. In fact, many of your friends and family who play golf will try diligently to "help." Unfortunately, what is good advice for one person may not work for someone else. Working with a PGA or LPGA teaching professional is the best way to learn the game. These accomplished instructors are required to complete a comprehensive program that spans several years before they become fully certified, so you can be sure that they know their craft!

Thousands of these pros work at public, resort, and private golf facilities, so getting access to them is not a problem. There are various ways to select an instructor:

- Ask someone who has taken lessons or has worked with a specific instructor for a recommendation.

- Refer to the popular golf magazines, such as *Golf Digest, GOLF Magazine,* and *Golf For Women,* and their lists of the top instructors. These teachers will charge the highest rates, but they also might be able to refer you to a less expensive local teacher they know.

- Search the listings on the PGA and LPGA websites. To find a PGA instructor in your area, go to www.pga.com, click on "Improve Your Game," and then click on "Find a PGA Instructor." To find an LPGA instructor, go to www.lpga.com and then click on "Find a Teacher."

- Call a nearby golf course and ask if they have instructors who give lessons. Ask to speak directly with the instructor and find out whether he or she is comfortable assisting beginning golfers. If you like the way the professional presents himself or herself, then book a lesson after checking out the lesson rates (which can vary greatly by instructor and golf course).

- If the prices are higher than what you expected, you can take a lesson with a PGA Apprentice. These pros-in-training frequently offer instruction at a lower rate because they have less experience. Or you can book a lesson with a friend and divide the cost between you if the teaching professional agrees to the arrangement.

## WHAT TO ASK THE INSTRUCTOR

Establishing a comfort level with an instructor is key to successful learning. To start the process, you should ask a number of questions before agreeing to take lessons with a particular pro:

- How long have you been teaching? (Experienced instructors have at least ten years on the job.)
- How much does a lesson cost?
- Do you offer a discount for a series of lessons? (Many pros offer six lessons for the price of five.)
- What form of payment is expected (credit card, personal checks, cash, etc.)?
- How long are the lessons? (Lessons usually come in 30-minute, 45-minute, or one-hour increments. Playing lessons, where the instructor accompanies you on the course to play a number of holes, can last longer. Playing lessons are a great way to put into practice what you have learned. They enable you to get comfortable on a golf course and remind you of the true object of the game—getting the ball into the hole!)
- When are you available to give a lesson?
- Will a video of our session be provided?

If you are contacting an instructor at a private golf club to which you do not belong, also make sure to ask if he or she teaches non-members.

## WHAT TO BRING TO A LESSON

Lessons aren't cheap, so you want to be prepared to get the most out of your time with the teaching pro. Ask the instructor what you are expected to bring to your first lesson. Here are some other questions you might ask:

- Where do I meet you at the course/facility?
- Do I need to wear golf shoes?
- Is there a dress code? (Asking this question is especially important at private clubs, which often have strict rules on golfers' attire.)
- Do I need to bring my own clubs? (Many facilities offer clubs that you can borrow at no charge for your lesson.)
- Can I bring a note pad, or will one be provided?

**TIP**

Don't hastily commit to a series of lessons. (Many facilities offer incentive-style packages.) Take a single 30-minute or one-hour lesson to start. Use it to meet the instructor, determine your comfort level with him or her, and discuss your goals. You should not book further lessons until you are comfortable with a particular instructor.

*CONTINUED ON NEXT PAGE*

## GOALS AND EXPECTATIONS

Although there are fundamentals of golf that all beginners must learn and your instructor will be happy to teach you, it is helpful to define your goals and expectations before you begin your lessons. Here are two questions to consider:

- **What do you expect to achieve in golf?** Maybe you want to learn to play golf for business purposes, or as a way to spend time with family or friends, or even to become a competitive player someday.

- **Do you have a specific goal in mind?** You might be looking to achieve a certain score, hit the ball farther than your buddies, fix that frustrating slice or hook, or simply be more consistent in all areas of the game.

Every person has different thoughts about what they want to accomplish, but none of them means much if you aren't having fun. That's why the most important goal of all should be enjoyment!

Remember, too, that certain sacrifices are required to become better and better. As champion golfer Gary Player once said, "The harder I practice, the luckier I get." Determining *realistic* goals is a collaborative effort between you and your instructor.

You may watch the pros on television or at a tournament and think that you could hit shots like they do with a little more practice. Keep in mind that they have spent their entire lives playing and practicing. If you hit 10 percent of your balls into the air during your first lessons, consider your lessons a success. At this point, you are simply trying to understand how to make a golf swing. As you learn, play, and practice, your skills will improve over time.

## ONE-ON-ONE LESSONS VERSUS CLINICS AND GOLF SCHOOLS

Clinics (even those that you set up on your own by taking a private lesson with some friends) offer a great way to get a taste of golf instruction—and to keep the initial costs down. But one-on-one lessons offer better results in the long run.

Golf schools are a wonderful experience for some people. Generally you attend for a day, a long weekend, or even a week. Because of the short period of time and the number of students, a lot of information is presented rather quickly. If you are interested in attending a golf clinic, research different options, get references, and make sure that the clinic you choose is run by a PGA or LPGA instructional staff.

**TIP**

The same etiquette applies both when you play and when you practice. Be respectful of other golfers and refrain from making unnecessary noise. On the range, never step out toward the landing area to grab a ball. On the putting green, try to hit to a hole not being used by others.

Go to any public driving range and you'll see people hitting buckets of balls for hours on end. Doing so can be fun, but will it help your golf game? Probably not. Practicing with a purpose, however, will make you a better player—and it can be just as fun. This section describes different ways to make your practice sessions more effective.

Always start a practice session by stretching for a few minutes before you hit any balls. (See Chapter 9 for recommended stretches.) If you are not focusing on anything specific, start with your wedges to work on your swing tempo and timing without worrying about distance. Then work your way through your clubs, eventually working your way up to your driver. End the session by hitting some more wedge shots to develop your touch and feel.

## USE TARGETS

Hitting ball after ball at nothing in particular may help you learn to strike the ball more consistently, but it will do nothing toward helping you make more accurate shots on the course, where your goal is to get the ball *into the hole*. That's why most practice ranges have greens with different colored flags on them that serve as targets. Try to find out the distance to each flag so that you can work on specific yardages and learn what clubs you can hit to that distance.

You don't need flags to aim at, though; pick a shadow out in the distance and aim for it, or use a section of discolored grass as your target. Or hit your first ball and then use that ball as your intended target.

## HIT ALL ODDS OR EVENS

Hitting practice shots with every single club in your bag will only tire you out. Instead, select a few clubs to work with in each practice session. For example, devote one practice session to using only your even-numbered irons (pitching wedge, 8-iron, and 6-iron), and try hitting them alternate distances to help you get a feel for different shots.

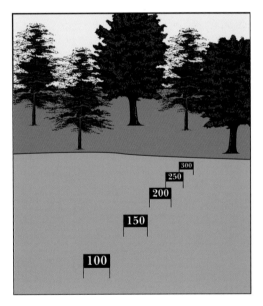

*CONTINUED ON NEXT PAGE*

## PLAY HOLES

Set aside ten balls from your bucket for the end of your practice session and use them as if you were playing the first three holes of the next course you will play. Visualize each hole and practice as if you actually were playing each shot on that hole. Wait 30 seconds or so between shots to help re-create the feel of being on the course, where you would be walking or riding to your next shot.

## WORK ON YOUR SHORT GAME

The majority of shots you take on a golf course are from 100 yards and in, so devote a practice session to using only your wedges. The better feel you have for these clubs, the better you will be able to get the ball close to the hole and improve your scores.

### TIP

Here are some other ideas to help you focus your practice sessions:

- **Play "Horse":** Basketball players often play "Horse" by experimenting with different shots. Miss a shot and you get assigned a letter. Get all the letters in HORSE and you're eliminated from the game. You can do the same thing at the driving range. Practice with a friend and call out different shots to hit. You could call for a certain distance, a target, or even the number of times the ball bounces before it stops. Doing so will help you create new shots while developing touch and feel with a variety of clubs.

- **Swing Music:** Many people wind up doing more talking than practicing at the driving range. Everyone likes to talk about the latest equipment, swing tip, or pro tournament results. But you should be there to focus on practice. Wearing headphones, with or without music playing, reinforces that message to people who might try to talk with you.

# Appendix A: PGA Sections

Working with a qualified golf teacher is a great way to learn how to play the game. The best sources for professional instructors are the PGA and LPGA, whose members undergo an extensive training program in order to become certified. To find a PGA or LPGA teaching professional near you, contact the appropriate office listed on the following pages, or go to www.pga.com or www.lpga.com for more information.

## ALOHA

770 Kapiolani Blvd., Suite 706
Honolulu, HI 96813
808-593-2230 (office)
877-742-6248 (toll-free)
808-593-2234 (fax)
aloha@pgahq.com
www.aloha.pga.com

## CAROLINAS

3852 Highway 9 East
P.O. Box 4567
N. Myrtle Beach, SC 29597-0709
843-399-2742 (office)
843-399-1504 (fax)
carolinas@pgahq.com
www.carolinas.pga.com

## CENTRAL NEW YORK

800 Nottingham Rd.
Syracuse, NY 13224
315-446-5610 (office)
315-446-5870 (fax)
crtrlny@pgahq.com
www.cny.pga.com

## COLORADO

6630 Bear Dance Rd., Suite 200
Larkspur, CO 80118
303-681-0742 (office)
888-987-2742 (toll-free)
303-681-3992 (fax)
colorado@pgahq.com
www.colorado.pga.com

## CONNECTICUT

35 Cold Spring Rd., Suite 212
Rocky Hill, CT 06067
860-257-4653 (office)
860-257-8355 (fax)
conn@pgahq.com
www.connecticut.pga.com

## DIXIE

1300 Ballantrae Club Dr.
Pelham, AL 35124
205-621-6401 (office)
205-664-3202 (fax)
dixie@pgahq.com
www.dixie.pga.com

## GATEWAY

17269 Wild Horse Creek Rd., Suite 110
Chesterfield, MO 63005
636-207-0795 (office)
636-207-0796 (fax)
gateway@pgahq.com
www.gatewaypga.org

## GEORGIA

590 W. Crossville Rd., Suite 204
Roswell, GA 30075
678-461-8600 (office)
678-461-0500 (fax)
georgia@pgahq.com
www.georgia.pga.com

## GULF STATES

10 Villere Dr.
P.O. Box 1266
Destrehan, LA 70047
985-725-1655 (office)
504-725-1176 (fax)
gulfstat@pgahq.com
www.gulfstates.pga.com

## ILLINOIS

2901 W. Lake Ave., Suite A
Glenview, IL 60025
847-729-5700 (office)
847-729-5599 (fax)
illinois@pgahq.com
www.ipga.com

## INDIANA

P.O. Box 516
Franklin, IN 46131
317-738-9696 (office)
800-779-7271 (toll-free)
317-738-9436 (fax)
indiana@indianagolf.org
www.indianagolf.org

## IOWA

1930 St. Andrews NE
Cedar Rapids, IA 52402
319-378-9142 (office)
319-378-9203 (fax)
iowa@pgahq.com
www.iowapga.com

## KENTUCKY

Golf House Kentucky
1116 Elmore Just Dr.
Louisville, KY 40245
502-243-8295 (office)
502-243-9266 (fax)
kentucky@pgahq.com
www.kentucky.pga.com

## METROPOLITAN NEW YORK

49 Knollwood Rd., Suite 200
Elmsford, NY 10523
914-347-2325 (office)
914-347-2014 (fax)
met@pgahq.com
www.met.pga.com

## MICHIGAN

P.O. Box 4399
East Lansing, MI 48826-4399
517-641-PGA1 (7421) (office)
517-641-7830 (fax)
www.michigan.pga.com

## MIDDLE ATLANTIC

1 PGA Dr.
Stafford, VA 22554
540-720-7420 (office)
540-720-7076 (fax)
midatl@pgahq.com
www.middleatlantic.pga.com

## MIDWEST

1960 NW Copper Oaks Circle
Blue Springs, MO 64015
816-229-6565 (office)
877-625-6565 (toll-free)
816-220-9644 (fax)
midwest@pgahq.com
www.midwest.pga.com

## MINNESOTA

12800 Bunker Prairie Rd.
Coon Rapids, MN 55448
763-754-0820 (office)
763-754-6682 (fax)
info@minnesotpga.com
www.minnesotpga.com

## NEBRASKA

8700 Executive Woods Dr., Suite 100
Lincoln, NE 68512
402-489-7760 (office)
402-489-1785 (fax)
nebraska@pgahq.com
www.nebraska.pga.com

## NEW ENGLAND

284 E. Temple St.
P.O. Box 743
Boylston, MA 01505
508-869-0000 (office)
508-869-0009 (fax)
neinfo@pgahq.com
www.newengland.pga.com

## NEW JERSEY

255 Old New Brunswick Rd., Suite 100 South
Piscataway, NJ 08854
732-465-1212 (office)
732-465-9524 (fax)
newjers@pgahq.com
www.newjersey.pga.com

## NORTH FLORIDA

200 Forest Lake Blvd., Suite 3
Daytona Beach, FL 32119
386-322-0899 (office)
386-322-2567 (fax)
NFlorida@PGAHQ.com
www.nfpga.com

## NORTHEAST NEW YORK

120 Russell Rd., Suite 2
Albany, NY 12205
518-438-8645 (office)
518-438-8670 (fax)
neny@pgahq.com
www.neny.pga.com

## NORTHERN CALIFORNIA

411 Davis St., Suite 103
Vacaville, CA 95688
707-449-4742 (office)
707-449-4755 (fax)
info@ncpga.com
www.ncpga.com

## NORTHERN OHIO

4735 Richmond Rd.
Warrensville Heights, OH 44128
216-765-1214 (office)
216-765-0639 (fax)
nohio@pgahq.com
www.northernohio.pga.com

## NORTHERN TEXAS

15150 Preston Rd., Suite 250
Dallas, TX 75248
214-420-7421 (office)
214-420-7424 (fax)
kwhittredge@ntpga.com
www.northerntexas.pga.com

## PACIFIC NORTHWEST

Dale Johnson Building
6989 Littlerock Rd. SW
Tumwater, WA 98512
360-456-6496 (office)
360-456-6745 (fax)
pacnw@pgahq.com
www.pnwpga.com

## PHILADELPHIA

715 Twining Rd., Suite 211
Dresher, PA 19025
215-886-7742 (office)
215-886-6742 (fax)
phil@pgahq.com
www.philadelphia.pga.com

## ROCKY MOUNTAIN

600 E. State St., Suite 300
Eagle, ID 83616
208-939-6028 (office)
208-939-6058 (fax)
rockymtn@pgahq.com
www.rockymountain.pga.com

## SOUTH CENTRAL

951 N. Forest Ridge Blvd.
Broken Arrow, OK 74014
918-357-3332 (office)
918-357-3328 (fax)
scentral@pgahq.com
www.southcentral.pga.com

## SOUTH FLORIDA

10045 Old Club Rd.

Parkland, FL 33076

954-752-9299 (office)

954-752-9659 (fax)

sflorida@pgahq.com

www.sflorida.pga.com

## SOUTHERN CALIFORNIA

36201 Champions Dr.

Beaumont, CA 92223

951-845-4653 (office)

951-769-6733 (fax)

scpga@pgahq.com

www.southerncal.pga.com

## SOUTHERN OHIO

101 E. Dayton – Yellow Springs Rd.

Fairborn, OH 45324

937-754-4263 (office)

937-754-4663 (fax)

sohio@pgahq.com

www.southernohio.pga.com

## SOUTHERN TEXAS

21604 Cypresswood Dr.

Spring, TX 77373

832-442-2404 (office)

832-442-2403 (fax)

stexas@pgahq.com

www.southerntexas.pga.com

## SOUTHWEST

10685 N. 69th St.

Scottsdale, AZ 85254

480-443-9002 (office)

800-688-0742 (toll-free)

480-443-9006 (fax)

swest@pgahq.com

www.southwest.pga.com

## SUN COUNTRY

290 Prarie Star Rd.

Bernalillo, NM 87004

505-867-4690 (office)

505-867-4695 (fax)

scountry@pgahq.com

www.suncountry.pga.com

## TENNESSEE

400 Franklin Rd.

Franklin, TN 37069

615-790-7600 (office)

615-790-8600 (fax)

dhorton@pgahq.com

www.golfhousetennessee.com

## TRI-STATE

221 Sherwood Dr.

Monaca, PA 15061

724-774-2224 (office)

724-774-5535 (fax)

tristate@pgahq.com

www.tristate.pga.com

## UTAH

2155 E. 3300 South

Salt Lake City, UT 84109

801-485-0465 (office)

801-485-1203 (fax)

utah@pgahq.com

www.utah.pga.com

## WESTERN NEW YORK

8265 Sheridan Dr.

Williamsville, NY 14221

716-626-0603 (office)

716-626-5308 (fax)

wnewyork@pgahq.com

www.westernnewyork.pga.com

## WISCONSIN

11350 W. Theo Trecker Way

West Allis, WI 53214

414-443-3570 (office)

414-443-0817 (fax)

wisc@pgahq.com

www.wisconsin.pga.com

# Appendix B: Glossary

**ace**   A hole-in-one.

**approach**   A shot taken with the intention of reaching the green.

**apron**   The closely mown area located in front of the putting surface.

**away**   The player whose ball is farthest from the hole is considered to be "away" and should play his or her shot before all others who are closer to the hole.

**back nine**   Usually the holes numbered 10–18 on a golf course, or the last nine holes played in a competitive round. Some courses start players off on the tenth tee, making holes 10–18 the front nine and holes 1–9 the back nine.

**backswing**   The first portion of the swing, in which the club moves from address to the top.

**balata**   A soft, rubber-like material once commonly used as the outer surface of a golf ball.

**bent grass**   A type of grass used on putting greens.

**Bermuda grass**   A type of grass used on putting greens. It is more resistant to heat than bent grass and also reflects more grain, which affects the way you read a green: If you are putting against the grain, the grass will look darker; if you are putting with the grain, the grass will look shiny and the ball will roll more quickly.

**best ball**   A commonly used format in which the lowest score, or best ball, of a foursome counts as the team's score for the hole. Best ball is different from a scramble because every player plays his or her own ball from tee to green throughout the round.

**birdie**   A score of one stroke less than the assigned par for a hole—for example, if you take four strokes to get the ball into the hole on a par-five, you score a birdie.

**bite**   The way a ball lands on the green and stops suddenly due to backspin.

**blind shot**   A shot in which you cannot see your intended landing area.

**bogey**   A score of one stroke more than the assigned par for a hole—for example, if you take six strokes to get the ball into the hole on a par-five, you score a bogey.

**break**   The amount of movement, or curvature, between your ball and the hole. The topography of a putting surface can force the ball to move in different directions.

**bunker**   A depression in the ground usually filled with sand (though sometimes with grass), found mostly around greens but also in and along fairways. Bunkers are intended to trap errant shots.

**caddie**   A person who carries a player's golf clubs during a round (and is usually paid for the effort). A caddy can also keep your clubs clean, provide yardages for shots, rake bunkers, and help you read greens.

**carry**   The distance a ball travels in the air.

**cast**   A type of clubhead made by pouring metal into a mold.

**casual water**   Standing water on the course that is outside a normal water hazard; typically a temporary situation, normally the result of rain or a sprinkler system.

**chip**   A low, rolling shot that travels farther on the ground than it does in the air. This shot is used to advance the ball a short distance (35 yards or less) onto the green from the fairway or the fringe around the green. You can also chip from the rough if you have a good lie there.

**choke down**   To move your hands from the end of the grip downward toward the lower portion of the grip.

**closed**   A position in which the clubface can end up when it impacts the ball. A closed clubface usually causes the ball to move left. The term *closed* can also refer to a type of stance.

**clubface**   The surface of the clubhead that is designed to make contact with the ball.

**clubhead**   The part of the club that hits the ball; it is connected to the shaft by the hosel.

**clubhouse**   The central building at a golf facility where you pay green fees; the clubhouse usually includes the pro shop, locker rooms, and restaurant.

**concede**   To allow your opponent to pick up the ball during match play when he or she has a short putt that you do not believe will be missed. By conceding the putt, you do not require your opponent to actually make the putt.

**cup**   The cylindrical hole in the green that supports the flagstick.

**dimples**   Small indentations found on the surface of a golf ball.

**divot**   A portion of turf torn from the ground by a golf swing; also refers to the mark left in the ground as a result.

**dogleg**   A par-four or par-five hole that bends dramatically to the right or left.

**downswing**   The portion of the swing where the club moves from its highest point to impact with the ball.

**draw**   A shot that curves from right to left in a controlled manner.

**drive**   The first shot on a par-four or par-five hole for which a driver is used. If the player uses a club other than a driver, this is called a tee shot.

**drive the green**   A very rare situation in which a tee shot reaches the green on a par-four or par-five. If you can do this, you probably don't need to be reading this book!

**driving range**   A place to hit practice shots. A driving range can be a stand-alone facility or located at a golf course.

**drop area**   A designated area on a golf course where you can drop a ball after hitting it into a water hazard or an environmentally sensitive area; the drop area is usually identified by a sign.

**eagle**   A score of two strokes less than the assigned par for a hole—for example, if you take three strokes to put the ball into the hole on a par-five, you score an eagle.

**fade**   A shot that curves from left to right in a controlled manner.

**fairway**   The closely mown turf that stretches between the tee and the green.

**false front**   A deceptive design feature used by course architects to make a green appear closer than it really is. The false front extends into the fairway, usually in a downward fashion, often causing golfers to misjudge the distance and hit balls short of the proper landing area.

**fat**   See "hit it fat."

**first cut**   The portion of rough immediately adjacent to the fairway; on the opposite side of the first cut is higher rough.

**flagstick**   The stick placed in the hole on each green. A flag is attached to the top of the stick to help players see the position of the hole from far away.

**flop shot**  A high, arcing shot that lands very softly with little roll. It is used mainly around greens to fly over bunkers or to reach a short-sided pin position (where the pin is close to the near edge of the green).

**follow-through**  The portion of the swing that occurs after the clubhead makes impact with the ball.

**fore**  The term shouted by golfers after they hit an off-target shot to warn other players of the approaching ball.

**forged**  The clubhead-making process in which a block of solid metal is shaved down to a certain shape; forged clubs are usually the most expensive type.

**four ball**  A format of play in which a foursome is divided into two-person teams. Each players hits his or her own ball, with the lower of the two scores (the "best ball") counting as the team's score for that hole. In match play, the team with the lower score on a hole wins the hole.

**foursome**  A group comprised of four golfers. Golf facilities typically prefer that people play in groups of four, especially when the course is busy.

**free drop**  A situation in which you can move the ball and drop it without penalty—for example, if your ball ends up in an area marked as ground under repair.

**fringe**  A portion of closely mown turf that encircles the putting surface; fringe grass is slightly higher than the green itself.

**front nine**  Usually the holes numbered 1–9 on a golf course, or the first nine holes played in a competitive round. Some courses start players off on the tenth tee, making holes 1–9 the back nine.

**gallery**  The people watching a golf tournament in person.

**gimme**  A short putt that is expected to be made.

**green**  The designated putting surface of each hole, where the flagstick and cup are located.

**green fee**  The amount a facility charges for playing a round of golf.

**ground the club**  To rest your club on the ground prior to making a swing. Grounding your club in a bunker is not permitted.

**ground under repair**  An area on a golf course usually marked by a sign or by lines painted on the ground. If your ball ends up inside such an area, you are allowed to pick it up and drop it outside of the area, but no closer to the hole, without incurring a penalty stroke.

**halve**   To record the same score as another player on a hole in match play; that hole is said to be halved. This term also refers to a match that ends in a draw and does not continue to sudden death.

**handicap**   A number created by converting your established Handicap Index into an appropriate Course Handicap (a number that indicates a golfer's ability level—the better you are, the lower this number will be) for each course you play.

**Handicap Index**   According to the USGA, "The number issued by your golf club, which represents your potential scoring ability; it is expressed as a number taken to one decimal place (i.e., 10.4)." This index enables golfers with different scoring abilities and skill levels to play one another and have a competitive match. Use the chart available at the course you are playing to convert your Handicap Index into a Course Handicap.

**hazard**   An obstacle on the course, such as water (pond, lake, stream) or sand (bunker), that can add extra strokes to your score, either via a penalty stroke or because additional shots are needed to exit the hazard.

**head cover**   An item typically found on drivers and woods that protects both the clubhead and the shaft of the club.

**heel**   The portion of the clubface that is closest to the shaft.

**hit it fat**   To hit the ground first and then the ball, causing the ball to travel a shorter distance than planned.

**hit it thin**   To strike the middle or equator of the ball with the leading edge of the club, causing it to stay low to the ground with very little spin. Sometimes a thin shot reaches the target.

**hole**   The 4¼-inch circle located on every green of a golf course.

**hole-in-one**   The rare situation in which you take a total of one stroke from the tee to get the ball into the hole. Also known as an "ace," it almost always happens on a par-three.

**hole out**   To finish a hole by knocking the ball into the cup.

**honors**   The right to tee off first. Whoever has the lowest score on a hole is assigned the "honors" of teeing off first on the next hole.

**hook**   An errant shot that curves sharply from right to left in an uncontrollable manner.

**hosel**   The part of the golf club that connects the shaft with the clubhead; sometimes referred to as the "neck" of the club.

**hybrid**   A golf club that blends elements of an iron and a fairway wood.

**impact**   The moment the clubhead makes contact with the ball.

**iron**   The name for a club other than a driver, wood, or putter, numbered 1–9, plus the pitching wedge, sand wedge, and lob wedge.

**lag**   A long putt not expected to be made, but that finishes close enough to the hole that the following putt is very makeable.

**lateral water hazard**   Defined by red stakes, a hazard found to the side of a fairway or green.

**lay up**   To hit the ball short of the target rather than try to cover the entire distance. A golfer typically makes this shot selection when facing a long distance to cover in order to decrease the margin of error.

**leader board**   A chart posted during a golf tournament to show which players are leading the event.

**lie**   The position of your ball on the ground.

**lift, clean, and place**   A rule applied during a round in which bad weather conditions are in effect; it allows players to pick up the ball, clean it, and place it on a better lie without penalty.

**links course**   A wide-open, usually treeless style of golf course; an authentic links course is built on sandy soil very close to the sea.

**lip**   The edge of the hole.

**lob wedge**   A highly lofted club (at least 58 degrees or more) used to hit the ball a short distance with great height.

**loft**   The angle of the clubface relative to the ground, measured in degrees. The greater the degree of loft, the higher the trajectory and the shorter the distance of that club.

**loose impediments**   Natural objects not deemed to be an integral part of the course—pine cones, twigs, leaves, and so on. A golfer may remove loose impediments that affect the shot or stance without penalty unless in a bunker or hazard.

**marker**   An object used to mark the position of the ball on the green. You use a marker when your ball is in the way of another player's putt, or when you want to pick up the ball to clean it.

**marshal**   The person whose job is to monitor the play of a particular hole, usually during a tournament.

**match play**   A competitive format in which one player competes against another, with individual scores determining who wins each hole. When one player has won more holes than there are holes left to play (e.g., the player is up five holes with four left to play), that player wins the match.

**misread**   To fail to understand the topography of the green, resulting in a missed putt.

**movable obstruction**   According to the USGA's *The Rules of Golf,* "Something (except for objects defining out of bounds or objects out of bounds) that may be moved without unreasonable effort, without unduly delaying play, and without causing damage to the course." Such objects include rakes, coffee cups, trash cans, and benches.

**mulligan**   An unofficial tradition of taking another shot if the first one is not to a player's liking. Mulligans are not accepted under the official rules of golf and cannot be taken during competition.

**nassau**   A form of betting that usually involves separate wagers on the front nine score, the back nine score, and the overall score.

**offset**   A clubhead whose leading edge is positioned behind the hosel.

**open**   A position in which the clubface can end up when it impacts the ball. An open clubface usually results in the ball moving to the right.

**pairing**   The person or people with whom you are assigned to play.

**par**   The number of strokes a scratch golfer (one with a Course Handicap of zero) should take to complete a hole.

**pin**   Also known as the flagstick, the pin is the target placed in each hole on the course. A flag is attached to the top of the pin to help players see the location of the pin from a distance.

**pin-high**   An approach shot that comes to rest perpendicular to the pin. A pin-high shot can be on or off the green.

**pitch**   A shot hit from around or close to the green that travels more through the air than it does on the ground. This shot helps your ball fly over bunkers, water, or rough to get close to the hole. Because you use a high-lofted club to play this shot, the ball retains extra spin, giving it both height and the ability to stop quickly once it lands instead of rolling along the green as a chip shot would.

**play through**   To step to the side and allow the player or group of players directly behind you on the course to move ahead on a hole to improve the pace of play; proper etiquette calls for faster players to play through.

**practice green**   A putting surface that is not part of the course where you can practice putts prior to or after your round.

**press**   A second wager often used with a nassau bet; typically a point in time when a player requests that a separate wager begin. For instance, if one player gets to the 6th tee down four holes, that player can ask to "press." Holes 7, 8, and 9 then become a separate match for an additional wager. An "automatic press" must be agreed upon prior to play beginning.

**private course**   A golf course that requires membership to play.

**pro-am**   An event, usually held the day before a tournament begins, in which professionals play with amateurs who have paid to participate.

**pro shop**   A golf course facility, often located within the clubhouse, where you pay green fees, reserve tee times, pay for practice balls, and buy food and merchandise.

**provisional ball**   A second ball hit when you think your original ball may be lost or out-of-bounds.

**public course**   A golf course that is open to the public and does not require membership to play.

**pull**   A shot that veers sharply left after impact.

**punch out**   To use an abbreviated backswing to move the ball into a better position and out of trouble. Punching out is often required when the ball is in heavy rough, underneath a tree, or in tall grass.

**push**   A shot that veers sharply right after impact.

**putt**   A stroke you take when the ball is on the green.

**range**   A term used to describe the driving range, where players go to hit practice shots.

**range finder**   A device used to calculate the yardage of a shot.

**ranger**   The person whose primary job is to ensure the proper pace of play on a golf course and oversee the needs of the players. Also called a marshal.

**read the green**   To analyze the shape and topography of the putting surface in order to control the speed and accuracy of a putt.

**red stakes**   Indicate a lateral water hazard located to the side of a fairway or green.

**regulation** The number of strokes required to land the ball on the putting surface within par minus two strokes (in one shot on a par-three, in two shots on a par-four, or in three shots on a par-five).

**release** When the ball hits the ground and moves forward; or to rotate the right hand over the left hand during the swing, which helps square the clubface.

**relief** Depending on the situation, a player can obtain relief with or without a penalty (for example, when a ball stops on a cart path or lands behind a tree).

**rough** High and often thick grass that borders the fairway and surrounds the green.

**round** 18 holes of golf (or nine holes on a nine-hole course).

**sand wedge** A highly lofted club (54 to 57 degrees) used to hit shots out of bunkers, short-distance shots from the fairway to the green, or shots from heavy rough.

**sandie** The act of taking one shot out of a bunker and then one putt on the green.

**scramble** A competitive format in which each player in the group hits a tee shot and all the players in the group use the best tee shot for the next shot; play continues in this fashion, with everyone in the group hitting shots from one location, until a putt is made.

**scratch golfer** A player with a zero handicap—that is, a really good player.

**second cut** A type of rough that is adjacent to the first cut but is higher and often thicker.

**semi-private course** A course that is open to the public but also offers memberships.

**shaft** The part of the club that connects the grip with the clubhead. It can be made of graphite or steel.

**shank** An errant shot hit off the hosel of the club; it usually travels almost 90 degrees to the right.

**short game** A term that describes the shots made close to or around the green, mainly during pitching and chipping.

**short-sided** A term used to describe a player who has missed the green to the side that gives him or her the least amount of putting surface on which to land a pitch shot.

**shotgun start**   A format used during a golf outing in which foursomes are assigned to various holes and start play at the same time: For example, you may begin on the 13th hole, which means that you conclude your 18-hole round on the 12th hole.

**skins**   A format of play that puts a prize ("skin") on each hole, with the lowest score on the hole winning the skin. If no player has the single lowest score, that skin carries over to the next hole, and so on. Whoever ends up with the most skins at the end of the round wins the predetermined reward.

**sleeve**   A box of golf balls (usually three balls).

**slice**   An errant shot that curves sharply from left to right in an uncontrollable manner.

**spin**   An important factor affecting the trajectory, distance, and accuracy of a golf shot. The angle of the club's impact imparts spin on the ball.

**starter**   The person positioned near the first tee at a golf course who assists players in beginning their rounds in a timely manner; also acts as the caddy master.

**stroke**   A swing taken with the intention of advancing the ball.

**stroke play**   A widely used competitive format in which a player's score equals the total number of strokes he or she has taken; the player with the fewest strokes wins. Also known as medal play.

**superintendent**   The person responsible for the maintenance of the course and grounds at a golf facility.

**sweet spot**   The center of the clubface.

**swing plane**   The path along which your club travels during the swing.

**tap-in**   A short putt that requires a simple tap to knock the ball into the hole.

**tee**   The closely mown, often raised section of a hole from which you hit your first shot on the hole. Also, a small object with a point at the bottom that is used to raise the ball up off the surface of the tee box.

**tee markers**   A pair of items that define the proper teeing area on each hole. You must tee up your ball between the markers or no more than two club lengths behind them.

**tee shot**   The first shot on a par-four or par-five hole for which a club other than a driver is used. If the player uses a driver, this shot is called a drive.

**thin**   See "hit it thin."

**tight**   Close to the hole.

**top**   To strike the top half of the ball with the leading edge of the club, causing topspin and forcing the ball to fall to the ground immediately rather than travel up into the air.

**turn**   The point at which you have completed the first nine holes of a course (the "front nine") and are ready to begin the second nine holes (the "back nine").

**unplayable lie**   A lie in which the ball has come to rest in a position (such as behind a large rock) from which it cannot be hit.

**up and down**   A two-shot sequence that typically occurs around the green after the approach shot has missed the green or landed in a bunker. The first shot is hit "up" onto the green, and the first putt then goes "down" into the hole. Also referred to as a "save."

**USGA**   The United States Golf Association, the governing body for the sport of golf in the U.S.; based in Far Hills, New Jersey.

**waggle**   The process of moving the club back and forth just prior to hitting the ball, which helps loosen up your arms and shoulders.

**water hazard**   A pond, stream, or other body of water on a golf course defined by a yellow or red stake.

**wedge**   A lofted club used for short-distance shots approaching the green.

**whiff**   To swing a club with the intention of hitting the ball but to miss it completely. A whiff counts as a stroke.

**white stakes**   Indicate an area that is out-of-bounds.

**winter rules**   A local rule put into effect when conditions require preferred lies without penalty (usually implemented during the winter months).

**wood**   A club with a large head made of wood or metal that is used for tee shots and long fairway shots. Woods are numbered 1, 3, and 5; 7 and 9 woods with greater loft are also available.

**yardage marker**   Indicates the distance, in yards, from a certain point to the green. A yardage marker may reflect the distance to the front, middle, and back of the green; if only one number appears, it refers to the center of the green. Yardage markers are placed on the fairway or on the cart path; yardages can also be marked on sprinkler heads. Common distances noted by markers are 200, 150, and 100 yards to the green.

**yellow stakes**   Indicate a water hazard on the course.

**yips**   A largely psychological condition that afflicts players who can't keep their hands and arms steady while putting (and sometimes chipping), resulting in consistently poor shots.

# Appendix C: Swing Sequences

A proper golf swing can be a true thing of beauty. These pages show you the essential points of the various swings you will use on the course.

**DRIVE**

## IRON SHOT

# Index

shamble game, 164
shoes, 37
short game practice, 200
shot and grip pressure, 44
shotgun start, 217
shoulder stretch, 145
shoulders, slices and, 169
sidehill lie, 187–189
skins game, 164
skulled shots, 181
sleeve, 217
slices
    cause, 168
    troubleshooting, 168–171
snowman score, 14
soft balls, 35
Solheim Cup, 6
Sorenstam, Annika, 8
spin, 217
square clubface, 54
St. Andrews golf course, 4
stableford game, 164
stance
    chipping, 91
    greenside bunker shot, 109
    objects affecting rule, 156
    pitching, 96–99
    proper, 49–50
    putting, 127–131
    swing, 59–60
standard bunker shot lies, 116
standard grip, 125
starters, course, 149
starting downswing, 80
steering clear of putting lines etiquette, 163
stretching, 144–147
stroke play, 164
strokes count, 10
strong hand position, 47
sunscreen, 148
superintendent, 217
sweet spot, 217
swing
    about, 58
    backswing, 62–66
    balance and posture, 60
    ball position, 59
    chipping, 92
    downswing, 67
    driving, 78–82
    finish, 71, 82
    follow-through, 70
    impact, 68–69, 81
    irons, 58
    pitching, 100–101
    posture, 60
    practice swing, 61
    putting, 132–133
    stance, 59–60, 78
    swing path, 72–73
swing music, 200

swing path
    inside-outside path, 73
    outside-inside path, 73
    proper path, 72
swinging club, greenside bunker shot, 110–113

## T

take aim, align shot, 52
targets, practice, 199
tee box
    about, 12
    driving, 77
tee shot routine, 84–85
teeing ball within tee markers rule, 153
tees, 9, 35, 76, 148
television, 5
tending flag, 154
three jack game, 164
tight, 218
top of backswing driving, 80
topping shots, 178–179, 218
torso stretch, 146–147
tournaments
    British Open, 6
    Masters, 6
    PGA Championship, 6
    Ryder Cup, 6
    scoring, 159
    team, 6
    U.S. Open, 6
towels, 39
travel for golf
    Bandon Dunes, OR, 23
    Hawaii, 21
    Hilton Head, SC, 24
    Kiawah Island, SC, 24
    local customs, 17
    Myrtle Beach, SC, 24
    Orlando, FL, 20
    Pebble Beach, CA, 19
    Pinehurst, NC, 22
    Scottsdale, AZ, 18
    seasons, 17
    tour operators, 17
    Whistling Straits, WI, 25
    World Golf Village, FL, 20
    yearly maintenance, 17
troubleshooting
    divots, 182
    hit off downhill lie, 190–191
    hit off sidehill lie, 187–189
    hit off uphill lie, 192–193
    hit out from under tree, 185
    hit out of deep rough, 186
    hit out of divot, 183
    hit up from against collar, 184
    hitting fat, 176–177
    hitting thin, 178–179
    hooked shots, 172–175
    line drives, 181

# Teach Yourself VISUALLY™ books...

Whether you want to knit, sew, or crochet...strum a guitar or play the piano...train a dog or create a scrapbook...make the most of Windows XP or touch up your Photoshop CS2 skills, Teach Yourself VISUALLY books get you into action instead of bogging you down in lengthy instructions. All Teach Yourself VISUALLY books are written by experts on the subject and feature:

• Hundreds of color photos or screenshots that demonstrate each step or skill

• Step-by-step instructions accompanying each photo
• FAQs that answer common questions and suggest solutions to common problems
• Information about each skill clearly presented on a two- or four-page spread so you can learn by seeing and doing
• A design that makes it easy to review a particular topic

Look for Teach Yourself VISUALLY books to help you learn a variety of skills—all with the proven visual learning approaches you enjoyed in this book.

0-7645-9641-1

## Teach Yourself VISUALLY™ Crocheting

Picture yourself crocheting accessories, garments, and great home décor items. It's a relaxing hobby, and this is the relaxing way to learn! This Visual guide *shows* you the basics, beginning with the tools and materials needed and the basic stitches, then progresses through following patterns, creating motifs and fun shapes, and finishing details. A variety of patterns gets you started, and more advanced patterns get you hooked!

0-7645-9640-3

## Teach Yourself VISUALLY™ Knitting

Get yourself some yarn and needles and get clicking! This Visual guide *shows* you the basics of knitting—photo by photo and stitch by stitch. You begin with the basic knit and purl patterns and advance to bobbles, knots, cables, openwork, and finishing techniques—knitting as you go. With fun, innovative patterns from top designer Sharon Turner, you'll be creating masterpieces in no time!

0-7645-9642-X

## Teach Yourself VISUALLY™ Guitar

Pick up this book and a guitar and start strumming! *Teach Yourself VISUALLY Guitar* shows you the basics photo by photo and note by note. You begin with essential chords and techniques and progress through suspensions, bass runs, hammer-ons, and barre chords. As you learn to read chord charts, tablature, and lead sheets, you can play any number of songs, from rock to folk to country. The chord chart and scale appendices are ready references for use long after you master the basics.